Lecture Notes in Computer Science 3517

Commenced Publication in 1973
Founding and Former Series Editors:
Gerhard Goos, Juris Hartmanis, and Jan van Leeuwen

T0232836

Henry S. Baird   Daniel P. Lopresti (Eds.)

Human
Interactive Proofs

Second International Workshop, HIP 2005
Bethlehem, PA, USA, May 19-20, 2005
Proceedings

 Springer

Volume Editors

Henry S. Baird
Daniel P. Lopresti
Lehigh University
Computer Science and Engineering Department
Bethlehem, Pennsylvania, USA
E-mail: {baird,lopresti}@cse.lehigh.edu

Library of Congress Control Number: 2005926089

CR Subject Classification (1998): I.4, I.5, H.4, C.2, D.4.6, K.4.4, K.6.5, H.3

ISSN   0302-9743
ISBN-10   3-540-26001-3 Springer Berlin Heidelberg New York
ISBN-13   978-3-540-26001-1 Springer Berlin Heidelberg New York

Springer is a part of Springer Science+Business Media

springeronline.com

© Springer-Verlag Berlin Heidelberg 2005
Printed in Germany

Typesetting: Camera-ready by author, data conversion by Boller Mediendesign
Printed on acid-free paper   SPIN: 11427896   06/3142   5 4 3 2 1 0

Preface

E-commerce services are suffering abuse by programs (bots, spiders, etc.) masquerading as legitimate human users. Efforts to defend against such attacks have, over the past several years, stimulated investigations into a new family of security protocols – "Human Interactive Proofs" (HIPs) – which allow a person to authenticate herself as a member of a given group: e.g., as a human (vs. a machine), as herself (vs. anyone else), as an adult (vs. a child). Most commercial uses of HIPs today are CAPTCHAs, "Completely Automatic Public Turing tests to tell Computers and Humans Apart," which exploit the gap in ability between humans and machine vision systems in reading images of text. HIP challenges can also be non-graphical, e.g., requiring recognition of speech, solving puzzles, etc.

We are pleased to present the first refereed and archivally published collection of state-of-the-art papers on HIPs and CAPTCHAs. Each paper was reviewed by three members of the Program Committee, judged by the Co-chairs to be of sufficient relevance and quality, and revised by the authors in response to the referees' suggestions.

The papers investigate performance analysis of novel CAPTCHAs, HIP architectures, and the role of HIPs within security systems. Kumar Chellapilla, Kevin Larson, Patrice Simard, and Mary Czerwinski describe user trials of a CAPTCHA designed to resist segmentation attacks, including a systematic evaluation of its tolerance by human users. Henry Baird, Michael Moll, and Sui-Yu Wang analyze data from a human legibility trial of another segmentation-resistant CAPTCHA and locate a highly legible engineering regime. Amalia Rusu and Venu Govindaraju describe research towards CAPTCHAs based on reading synthetically damaged images of real images of unconstrained handwritten text. Yong Rui, Zicheng Liu, Shannon Kallin, Gavin Janke, and Cem Paya discuss the results of experiments with human subjects presented with two kinds of CAPTCHAs: one based on reading text, and a new one based on the detection of well-formed synthetic faces.

Monica Chew and J.D. Tygar discuss collaborative filtering CAPTCHAs which do not depend on absolute answers, but are graded by comparison with other people's answers. Tim Converse proposes CAPTCHA generation as a not-for-profit Web service and argues for open-sourcing the code. Daniel Lopresti proposes using instances of open pattern recognition problems to build CAPTCHAs in order to benefit both online security and pattern recognition research.

Jon Bentley and Colin Mallows describe methods for quantifying the assurance that can be inferred from a correct answer to a password query: the principles underlying this analysis are applicable to the evaluation of CAPTCHA security. Rachna Dhamija and J.D. Tygar investigate HIPs in which a user issues challenges to the computer, rather than the other way around, enabling the detection of phishing attacks.

We are warmly grateful for the time and skill volunteered by our Program Committee, as well as to our Advisory Board for kindly assisting in publicizing the event and suggesting ways to make the program more stimulating.

May 2005

Henry S. Baird
Daniel P. Lopresti
Workshop Co-chairs, HIP 2005
Department of Computer Science & Engineering
Lehigh University
Bethlehem, PA, USA

Organization

HIP 2005 was organized by the Department of Computer Science & Engineering, Lehigh University and was endorsed by IAPR, the International Association for Pattern Recognition.

Advisory Board

Jon Bentley	Avaya Labs Research
Manuel Blum	Computer Science, Carnegie-Mellon University
Andrei Broder	IBM Research
Gordon Legge	Psychology Depts., University of Minnesota
Richard Lipton	College of Computing, Georgia Tech
Patrice Simard	Microsoft Research
Doug Tygar	Computer Science & SIMS Depts., UC Berkeley

Program Committee

Luis von Ahn	Computer Science, Carnegie-Mellon University
Kumar Chellapilla	Microsoft Research
Monica Chew	Computer Science, UC Berkeley
James Clark	ECE Dept, McGill University
Brian Davison	Computer Science & Engineering, Lehigh
Irfan Essa	GVU Center, Georgia Tech
Venugopal Govindaraju	CEDAR, SUNY Buffalo
Greg Kochanski	Phonetics Lab, Oxford University
Richard Landsman	America Online
Cem Paya	Microsoft MSN/Passport
David Pletcher	Lawrence Livermore Lab, Berkeley
Chilin Shih	EALC & Linguistics, University of Illinois
Richard Sproat	Linguistics & ECE, University of Illinois

Sponsoring Institutions

We gratefully acknowledge financial support from Microsoft Research and Avaya Labs Research.

Table of Contents

CAPTCHAs and Performance Analysis

Building Segmentation Based Human-Friendly Human Interaction
Proofs (HIPs) 1
*K. Chellapilla, K. Larson, P.Y. Simard, and M. Czerwinski
(Microsoft Research)*

A Highly Legible CAPTCHA That Resists Segmentation Attacks 27
H.S. Baird, M.A. Moll, and S.-Y. Wang (Lehigh University)

Visual CAPTCHA with Handwritten Image Analysis 42
A. Rusu and V. Govindaraju (University at Buffalo)

Characters or Faces: A User Study on Ease of Use for HIPs 53
Y. Rui, Z. Liu, S. Kallin, G. Janke, and C. Paya (Microsoft)

HIP Architectures

Collaborative Filtering CAPTCHAs 66
M. Chew and J.D. Tygar (University of California at Berkeley)

CAPTCHA Generation as a Web Service 82
T. Converse (Yahoo!)

Leveraging the CAPTCHA Problem 97
D. Lopresti (Lehigh University)

HIPs Within Security Systems

How Much Assurance Does a PIN Provide? 111
J. Bentley and C. Mallows (Avaya Labs Research)

Phish and HIPs: Human Interactive Proofs to Detect Phishing Attacks .. 127
R. Dhamija and J.D. Tygar (University of California at Berkeley)

Author Index 143

Building Segmentation Based Human-Friendly Human Interaction Proofs (HIPs)

Kumar Chellapilla, Kevin Larson, Patrice Y. Simard, and Mary Czerwinski

Microsoft Research, One Microsoft Way, Redmond, WA, USA 98052
{kumarc, kevlar, patrice, marycz}@microsoft.com

Abstract. Human interaction proofs (HIPs) have become common place on the internet due to their effectiveness in deterring automated abuse of online services intended for humans. However, there is a co-evolutionary arms race in progress and these proofs are becoming more difficult for genuine users while attackers are getting better at breaking existing HIPs. We studied various popular HIPs on the internet to understand their strength and human friendliness. To determine HIP strength, we adopted a direct approach of building computer attacks using image processing and machine learning techniques. To understand human-friendliness, a sequence of users studies were conducted to investigate HIP character recognition by humans under a variety of visual distortions and clutter commonly employed in reading-based HIPs. We found that many of the online HIPs are pure recognition tasks that can be easily broken using machine learning. The stronger HIPs tend to pose a combination of segmentation and recognition challenges. Further, the HIP user studies show that given correct segmentation, computers are much better at HIP character recognition than humans. In light of these results, we propose that segmentation-based reading challenges are the future for building stronger human-friendly HIPs. An example of such a segmentation-based HIP is presented with a preliminary assessment of its strength and human-friendliness.

1 Introduction

Human Interaction Proofs[1] (HIPs) [3] or Completed Automated Public Turing tests to tell Computers and Humans Apart (CAPTCHAs) [4] are systems that allow a computer to distinguish between another computer and a human. These systems enable the construction of automatic filters that can be used to prevent automated scripts from utilizing services intended for humans [4]. An overview of the work in this area can be found in [3]. Work on building HIPs dates back to 1997 with the first HIP being invented [13] at the DEC Systems Research Center for blocking abusive automatic submission of URLs to the AltaVista web-site (www.altavista.com). Since then numerous HIPs have been proposed and several have been adopted by companies to

---

[1] These are also referred to as "Human Interactive Proofs." The term "Human Interaction Proof" is preferred in this paper as it is clearer in indicating that these are tests for human interaction.

H.S. Baird and D.P. Lopresti (Eds.): HIP 2005, LNCS 3517, pp. 1-26, 2005.

protect various services on the web. However, the basic challenge still remains the same: design a computer program that can automatically generate and grade tests that most humans can pass but current computer programs cannot pass. For a HIP to be successful in practice, it should also be fast and be capable of generating millions of unique samples a day.

Construction of HIPs of practical value is difficult because it is not sufficient to develop challenges at which humans are somewhat more successful than machines. This is because the cost of failure from using machines to solve the puzzles may be very small. In practice, if one wants to block automated scripts, a challenge at which humans are about 90% successful and machines are 1% successful, may not be sufficient, especially when the cost of failure and repetition is low for the machine [2,7,12]. At the same time, the identical challenge must not put too much burden on the human in order to avoid discouraging the use of the service. This is summarized in Figure 1. The figure shows an ideal distribution of HIPs. The sweet spot, where the HIPs are easy for humans to recognize but difficult for hackers to crack, is not guaranteed to actually exist. Furthermore, automatically generated HIPs, being random in nature, will have a distribution of difficulty, with some particular instances extending beyond the hypothesized sweet spot.

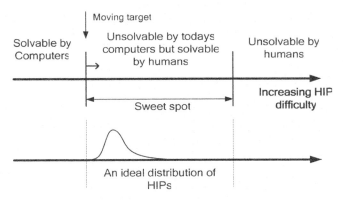

Fig. 1. Regions of feasibility as a function of HIP difficulty for humans and computers algorithms.

Depending on the cost of the attack and the value of the service, automatic scripts should not be more successful than 1 in 10,000 (0.01%). For good usability the human success rate should approach 90%. While the latter is a common requirement for reducing the number of retries a human user has to endure, the former is obtained by analyzing the cost of hiring humans to solve HIPs. For example, requiring a signup HIP for creating an e-mail account only imposes a maximal cost of about .002 cents per message, while the minimum estimate for the costs/potential revenue from sending spam are around .0025 cents, with many spammers charging or earning 5 to 10 times that [12]. Thus, a practical HIP must not only be secure but also be human-friendly. Human-friendliness encompasses both a) the visual appeal and annoyance factor of a HIP, and also b) how well it utilizes the difference in ability between humans and machines at solving segmentation and recognition tasks. While HIP security considerations push designers to make the HIP difficult for both humans and computers, the human-friendliness requirements force the designer to make them only as hard as they need to be and still be effective at deterring abuse. Due to this inherent conflict between these two requirements, online HIPs are undergoing an arms race. As computer vision research advances, computers get faster, and attackers get sophisticated, existing HIPs will become ineffective and new HIPs will have to be created. Over time, the sweet spot will decrease in size. Unfortunately, humans are unlikely to get better at solving HIPs in the same timeframe [10,11].

Owing to their advantages, reading-based HIPs have become common place for protecting internet web sites against abuse. Section 2 presents motivations for a reading-based HIP and several examples of common reading-based HIPs that can be sampled on the web. It also presents the segmentation and recognition parts of the HIP challenge and key design choices that go into building a reading-based HIP. Section 3 addresses HIP security from the point of view of a computer attacker attempting to solve a HIP completely (both segmentation and recognition parts being solved) or simply the recognition part of the problem. Section 4 investigates human-friendliness of a HIP by understanding human ability in solving HIP segmentation and recognition. Section 5 reviews lessons learned from computer attacks and user studies and presents segmentation-based HIPs. A preliminary analysis of the security and human-friendliness of an example segmentation-based HIP is also presented.

2   Examples of HIPs

We have come across dozens of proposals for HIP designs, ranging from counting objects in a picture, segmenting faces, recognizing animations, identifying words in audio, etc. [4]. Among visual challenges, Reading-based HIPs are the most obvious favorite [4,5,8,12,13,14]. These HIPs are made of characters rendered to an image and distorted before being presented to the user. Solving the HIP requires identifying all characters in the correct order. Several reasons for their popularity are:

1)   optical character recognition (OCR) is a well studied field and the state of the art is well known,

2)   characters were designed by humans for humans and humans have been trained at the task since childhood,

3)   each character has a corresponding key on the keyboard and 8 keystrokes span a space of over 1000 billion solutions,

4)   localization issues are minimal using western characters and numbers (without dictionaries),

5)   the task is easily understood by users without much instruction, and

6)   character-based HIPs can be generated quickly[2].

Figure 2 presents reading based HIPs that can be sampled from the web while signing up for free e-mail accounts with Mailblocks (www.mailblocks.com), MSN/Hotmail (www.hotmail.com), Yahoo! (www.yahoo.com), Google (gmail.google.com), run-

---

[2] Over 300 8-character HIPs can be generated per second on a 3GHz P4 [2,12]

ning a whois query at Register.com (www.register.com) or searching for tickets at Ticketmaster (www.ticketmaster.com), etc.

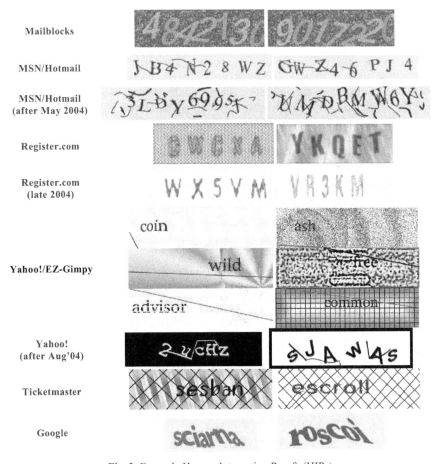

Fig. 2. Example Human Interaction Proofs (HIPs).

Solutions to Yahoo (ver1) HIPs are common English words, but those for ticketmaster and Google do not necessarily belong to the English dictionary. They appear to have been created using a phonetic generator [8]. Examining the changes in MSN, Yahoo!, and Register.com HIPs, we note that these HIPs are becoming progressively more difficult. While MSN introduced more arcs as clutter, Yahoo! gave up their language model and replaced simple textures and grids with more random intersecting lines and arcs. Register.com's update was relatively minor as they simply introduced digits into their character set.

2.1 Segmentation and Recognition Challenges

Reading-based HIP challenges typically comprise a segmentation challenge followed by recognition challenges[3]. Solving the segmentation challenge requires the identification of character locations in the right order. The random location of characters, background textures, foreground and background grids or lines, and clutter in the form of arcs make the segmentation problem difficult. Image warp exacerbates the segmentation problem by reducing the effectiveness of preprocessing stages of a segmentation algorithm that attempt to estimate and remove the background textures and foreground lines, etc. Once character locations are reliably identified (in the right order) each of the characters needs to be recognized correctly giving rise to the recognition problem. The character recognition problem is made difficult through changes in scale, rotation, local and global warp, and intersecting random arcs.

2.2 HIP Design Choices

While the segmentation and recognition challenges provide a conceptual breakdown of the HIP challenge, building an actual reading-based HIP requires one to make several independent choices:

a) **Character set**: The character set to be used in the HIP.

b) **Affine transformations**: Translation, rotation, and scaling of characters

c) **Adversarial clutter**: Random arcs, lines, or other simple geometric shapes that intersect with the characters and themselves

d) **Image warp:** elastic deformations of the HIP Image at different scales i.e., those that stretch and bend the character itself (global warp) and those that simply jiggle the character pixels (local warp)

e) **Background and foreground textures**: These textures are used to form a colored HIP image from a bi-level or grayscale HIP mask generated by using a) through d)

f) **Language model**: the language model determines both the conditional and joint probabilities of character co-occurrence in the HIP. A HIP can use a) no language model (random equally likely occurrence of all possible combinations – Eg. Mailblocks, MSN, Register and Yahoo version 2), b) words from a dictionary (Yahoo! version 1), or c) a phonetic generator [8] (Ticketmaster and Google/Gmail).

Each of these choices affects both HIP security and human-friendliness of the HIP though commonly to different degrees.

---

[3] Solving a HIP need not require the segmentation and recognition problems to be solved separately.

3   HIP Security

Assessing the strength of a particular HIP is an approximate process at best. The strength of a HIP is determined by the cumulative effects of the HIP design choices. Each choice increases or decreases HIP difficulty and human-friendliness. However, comparing and quantifying contributions from each choice might not be possible as interactions between these choices can be non-linear. Some very general comments can however be made. In general, the larger the character set and the longer the HIP the stronger it is. In the absence of a language model, the strength of the HIP improves exponentially with the length of the HIP and polynomially with the HIP character set size. Affine transformations, clutter, and image warp also increase HIP security through not as dramatically. Background and foreground textures usually provide only a marginal improvement in HIP security. Using only words from a dictionary makes the HIP considerably easier to break. HIPs using phonetic generators also suffer from this drawback but to a lesser extent. The effects of using a dictionary or a phonetic generator are similar to reducing the effective character set size and HIP solution length.

One direct approach to obtaining a quantitative upper bound for HIP security is to build automated HIP breakers and assess their success in solving particular HIPs. This is exactly the approach adopted here to assess HIP security for popular on-line HIPs [2,12].

3.1   Breaking HIPs

Breaking HIPs is not new. Mori and Malik [7] have successfully broken the EZ-Gimpy (92% success) and Gimpy (33% success) HIPs from CMU. Thayananthan et al [15] have also been successful at breaking EZ-Gimpy [4]. Recently Moy et al [16] have broken the purely distortion based HIP gimpy-r [4] with a success rate of 78%. Our approach aims at an automatic process for solving multiple HIPs with minimum human intervention, using machine learning. In this section, our main goal is to learn more about the common strengths and weaknesses of these HIPs rather than to prove that we can break any one HIP in particular with the highest possible success rate. We summarize results for six different HIPs: EZ-Gimpy/Yahoo, Yahoo v2, Mailblocks, Register, Ticketmaster, and Google. Further details on these HIP breakers can be found in [2,12].

To simplify our study, we will not be using language models in our attempt to break HIPs. For example, there are only about 561 words in the EZ-Gimpy dictionary [7], which means that a random guess attack would get a success rate of 1 in 561 (more than enough to break the HIP, i.e., greater than 0.01% success).

Our generic method for breaking all of these HIPs is to build a custom segmentation algorithm (to locate the characters) and then use machine learning for recognition. Surprisingly, segmentation, or finding the characters, is simple for many HIPs, which makes the process of breaking the HIP particularly easy. Gimpy uses a single constant predictable color (black) for letters even though the background color changes. We quickly realized that once the segmentation problem is solved, solving the HIP becomes a pure recognition problem, and it can be solved using machine learning. Our recognition engine is based on convolutional neural networks [6,9]. It yielded a 0.4% error rate on the MNIST database, uses little memory, and is very fast for recognition. Speed is important for breaking HIPs since it reduces the cost of automatic trials.

For each HIP, we have a segmentation step, followed by a recognition step. It should be stressed that we are not trying to solve every HIP of a given type, i.e., our goal is not 100% success rate, but something efficient that can achieve much better than 0.01%.

In each of the following HIP security experiments, 2500 HIPs were hand labeled and used as follows (a) recognition (1600 for training, 200 for validation, and 200 for testing), and (b) segmentation (500 for testing segmentation). For each of the five HIP types, a convolution neural network was trained and tested on gray level character images centered on the guessed character positions (see below). The convolutional neural network is identical to the one described in [6] and consisted of two layers of convolutional nodes followed by two fully connected layers. The output from each convolutional layer was subsampled by two before being fed to the next layer [6]. The architecture was exactly the same for all experiments in this paper. The trained neural network became the recognizer. Except for converting the original image to gray, **no preprocessing of any kind was used for recognition**.

Mailblocks: To solve the HIP, we select the red channel, binarize and erode it, extract the largest connected components (CCs), and breakup CCs that are too large into two or three adjacent CCs. Further, vertically overlapping half character sized CCs are merged. The resulting rough segmentation works most of the time. One example is presented in Figure 3.

Fig. 3. Breaking Mailblocks HIP.

In the example above, the neural network would be trained, and tested on the segmented chars (right). Each HIP has exactly 7 characters. The segmentation algorithm had a success rate of 88.8% and the neural network recognition rate was 95.9% for recognition (given correct segmentation). The total end-to-end success rate is given by `seg_rate*(reco_rate)^(hip_length)` = $(0.888)*(0.959)^7 = 66.2\%$ total. Note that most of the errors come from segmentation, even though this is where all the custom programming was invested.

Register: The procedure to solve HIPs is very similar. The image was smoothed, binarized, and the largest 5 connected components were identified. The success rate is 95.4% for segmentation, 87.1% for recognition (given correct segmentation), and $(0.954)*(0.871)^5 = 47.8\%$ total. One example is presented in Figure 4.

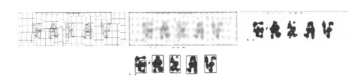

Fig. 4. Breaking Register HIP.

Yahoo!/EZ-Gimpy: Unlike the mailblocks and register HIPs, the Yahoo/EZ-Gimpy HIPs are richer in that a variety of backgrounds and clutter are possible. Though some amount of text warping is present, the text color, size, and font have low variability. Three simple segmentation algorithms were designed with associated rules to identify which algorithm to use. The goal was to keep these simple yet effective:

a) **No mesh**: Convert to grayscale image, threshold to black and white, select large CCs with sizes close to HIP char sizes. Figure 5 shows one example.

Fig. 5. Breaking Yahoo HIP: no mesh case.

b) **Black mesh**: Convert to grayscale image, threshold to black and white, remove vertical and horizontal line pixels that don't have neighboring pixels, select large CCs with sizes close to HIP char sizes. Figure 6 shows one example.

Fig. 6. Breaking Yahoo HIP: black mesh case.

c) **White mesh**: Convert to grayscale image, threshold to black and white, add black pixels (in white line locations) if there exist neighboring pixels, select large CCs with sizes close to HIP char sizes. Figure 7 shows one example.

Fig. 7. Breaking Yahoo HIP: black mesh case.

Tests for black and white meshes were performed to determine which segmentation algorithm to use. The average length of a Yahoo HIP solution is 4.8 characters. The end-to-end success rate was 56.2% for segmentation (38.2% came from a), 11.8% from b), and 6.2% from c), 90.3% for recognition (given correct segmentation), and $(0.562)*(0.903)^{4.8} = 34.4\%$ total. Note that the same recognizer was used for all 3 scenarios.

Ticketmaster: The procedure that solved the Yahoo HIP is fairly successful at solving some of the ticket master HIPs. These HIPs are characterized by cris-crossing lines at random angles clustered around 0, 45, 90, and 135 degrees. A multipronged attack as in the Yahoo case (section 3.3) has potential. In the interests of simplicity, a single attack was developed: Convert to grayscale, threshold to black and white, up-sample image, dilate first then erode, select large CCs with sizes close to HIP char sizes. One example is presented in Figure 8.

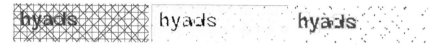

Fig. 8. Breaking Ticketmaster HIP.

The dilate-erode combination causes the lines to be removed (along with any thin objects) but retains solid thick characters. This single attack is successful in achieving an end-to-end success rate of 16.6% for segmentation, the recognition rate was 82.3% (in spite of interfering lines), and $(0.166)*(0.823)^{6.23} = 4.9\%$ total. The average HIP solution length is 6.23 characters.

Yahoo! (version 2): The second generation HIP from Yahoo had several changes: a) it did not use words from a dictionary or even use a phonetic generator, b) it uses only black and white colors, c) uses both letters and digits, and d) uses connected lines and arcs as clutter. The HIP is somewhat similar to the MSN/Passport HIP which does not use a dictionary, uses two colors, uses letters and digits, and back-ground and foreground arcs as clutter. Unlike the MSN/Passport HIP, several differ-ent fonts are used. A single segmentation attack was developed: Remove the 6 pixel border, up-sample, dilate first then erode, select large CCs with sizes close to HIP character sizes. The attack is practically identical to that used for the ticketmaster HIP with different preprocessing stages and slightly modified parameters. Figure 9 shows an example.

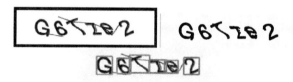

Fig. 9. Breaking Yahoo! (version 2) HIP.

This single attack is successful in achieving an end-to-end success rate of 58.4% for segmentation, the recognition rate was 95.2%, and $(0.584)*(0.952)^5 = 45.7\%$ total. The average HIP solution length is 5 characters.

Google/Gmail: The Google HIP is unique in that it uses only image warp as a means of distorting the characters. Similar to the MSN/Passport and Yahoo version 2 HIPs, it is also two colors. The HIP characters are arranged close to one another (they often touch) and follow a curved baseline. The following very simple attack was used to segment Google HIPs: Convert to grayscale, up-sample, threshold and separate connected components.

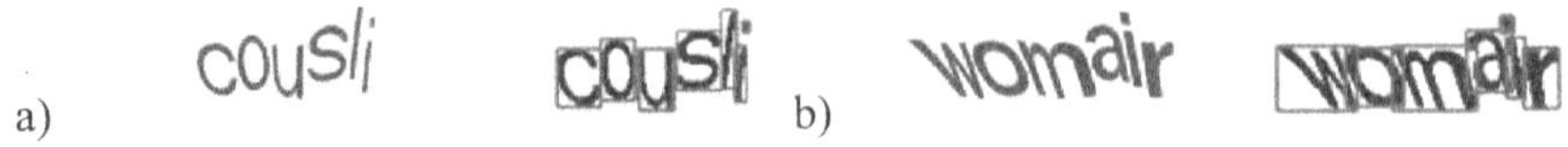

a)   *cousli*   *cousli* b)   *womair*   *womair*

Fig. 10. Breaking Google HIP.

This very simple attack gives an end-to-end success rate of 10.2% for segmentation, the recognition rate was 89.3%, giving $(0.102)*(0.893)^{6.5} = 4.89\%$ total probability of breaking a HIP. Average Google HIP solution length is 6.5 characters. This can be significantly improved upon by judicious use of dilate-erode attack. A direct application doesn't do as well as it did on the ticketmaster and yahoo HIPs (because of the shear and warp of the baseline of the word). More successful and complicated attacks might estimate and counter the shear and warp of the baseline to achieve better success rates.

The above experiments show that using a very simple approach, even the strongest HIPs can be solved more often than 1 in 25 leaving us far from the 1 in 10,000 mark. While recognition success rates ranged from 82.3% (ticketmaster) to 95.9% (mailblocks), segmentation success rates ranged from 10.2% (Google) to 95.4% (Register.com). Clearly, the segmentation problem is crucial in determining HIP security, while recognition of HIPs characters appears to be a solved problem.

3.2   Single Character Recognition Using Machine Learning

Interestingly, the recognition problems posed by the HIPs in Section 3.1 were specifically designed to fool off-the-shelf OCR systems (e.g. Scansoft's OCR and several others [14]). However, as seen in Section 3.1 they can be effectively solved using a neural network that is trained on HIP characters. In this section we explore the abilities of such a neural network [6] for solving single character recognition problems under a variety of distortions and clutter. These distortions are similar to those commonly employed in HIPs and are described below. In this study, to better understand the NN's capabilities, the difficulty of the recognition problem is driven much higher than what would be deemed appropriate for use in a HIP.

3.2.1   Single Character Recognition Using Machine Learning
Character-based HIPs employ a set of character distortions to make them hard to OCR using computers. The basic character transformations include translation, rotation (clockwise or counterclockwise), and scaling. Rotation is usually less than 45 degrees to avoid converting a 6 into a 9, an M into a W etc. Examples of these distortions are presented in figures 11, 12, and 13.

M7F47VWC

Fig. 11. Example of Plain Text (M7F47VWC)

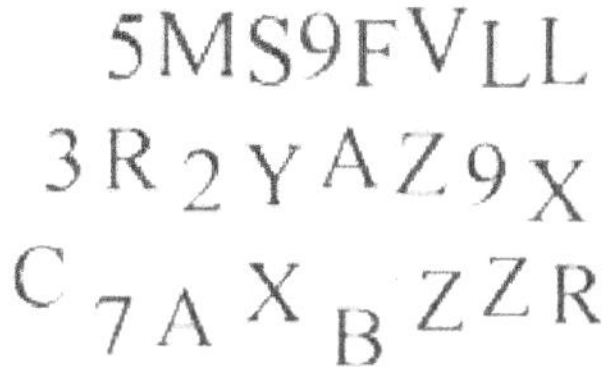

$$5MS9FVLL$$
$$3R_2YAZ9_X$$
$$C_{7A}X_BZZR$$

Fig. 12. Example of Translated Text, levels 10 (5MS9FVLL), 25 (3R2YAZ9X), and 40 (C7AXBZZR)

Fig. 13. Example of Rotation Text, levels 15 (PWVDYLVH), 30 (B5PYMMLB), and 45 (GSB5776E)

Both computers and humans find HIPs, using these three transformations, easy to solve. To increase the difficulty of computer-based OCR, we introduce two kinds of warp [17]:

1. **Global Warp**: The global warp produces character-level, elastic deformations (Figure 14). It is obtained by generating a random displacement field followed by a low pass filter with an exponential decay [17]. The resulting displacement field is then applied to the image with interpolation. These appear to bend and stretch the given characters. The magnitude of the warp is proportional to the total displacement distance of HIP image pixels. The purpose of these elastic deformations is to foil template matching algorithms.

2. **Local Warp**: Local warp is intended to produce small ripples, waves, and elastic deformations along the pixels of the character, i.e., at the scale of the thickness of the characters, rather than the scale of the width and height of the character (Figure 15). The local warp deformations are generated in the same manner as the global warp deformations, by changing the low pass filter cut-off to a higher frequency. The purpose of the local warp is to foil feature-based algorithms which may use character thickness or serif features to detect and recognize characters.

Crisscrossing straight lines and arcs, background textures, and meshes in foreground and background colors are common examples of clutter used in HIPs. In this paper, we used random arcs of different thicknesses as clutter.

Letter M under global warp

Left to right, letter M with varying amounts of global warp 75, 120, 180, 240, 300 respectively.

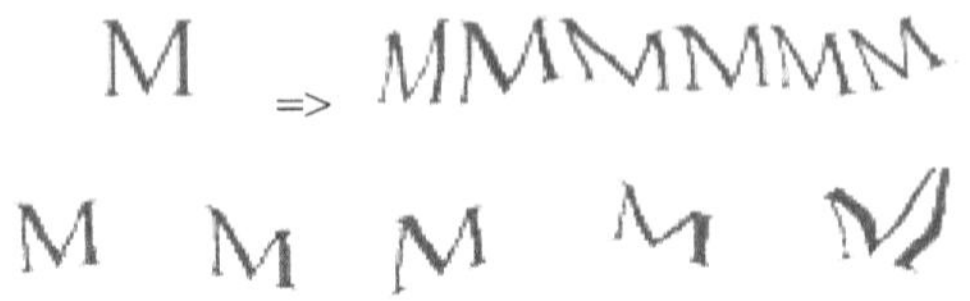

M => MMMMMM

M M M M M

Fig. 14. Character transformation under global warp.

Letter M under local warp

Left to right, letter M with varying amounts of local warp 20, 40, 60, and 80, respectively.

M => MMMMMM

M M M M

Fig. 15. Character transformation under local warp.

3.2.2   Single Character Recognition Using Machine Learning

We carried out a series of experiments to determine the recognition rates of the neural network classifier under the above distortions and clutter. In each experiment, a total of 110,000 random characters were sampled using the distortion and clutter settings. 90,000 characters were used for training and 10,000 were used for validation. Test error was computed over the remaining 10,000 characters. Thirty one characters from {A-Z, 0-9} were chosen. Five characters that can be easily confused were discarded. These were I, O, Q, 0, and 1. Characters were rendered in Times Roman font at font size 30.

In this paper, distortion and clutter were added to HIPs in the following order a) characters were rendered at random locations (with translation and rotation), b) foreground non-intersecting clutter (thick arcs that do not intersect) was rendered, c) foreground intersecting clutter (thin and thick foreground arcs that intersect), d) background intersecting clutter (thin and thick background arcs) and finally e) global and local warps were applied.

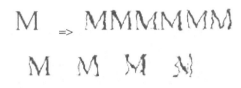

Fig. 16. Example of Baseline rotation, translation and scale for studying local warp and arc clutter.

The first three experiments studied rotation, global warp, and local warp in isolation. In the first experiment, characters were rotated randomly over the range of -45 to +45 degrees. In the second experiment, global warp was varied from 120 to 360 in steps of 60. For each setting a new neural network was trained. The third experiment studied recognition accuracy as local warp was varied from 20 to 80 in steps of 20. The fourth experiment was designed to explore the combined effect of simultaneously using these distortions and to provide a baseline for clutter experiments. The baseline setting used 80% - 120% scaling (x-, y-, or both), -20 to +20 degrees of rotation, a global warp setting of 75, and a local warp setting of 20. The fourth experiment used the baseline setting and the local warp was varied from 20 to 80 in steps of 20.

Single character neural network recognition results (on the test set) under different types of distortion are presented in Table 1. The NN accuracy was completely immune to rotation (with zero percent error), followed by local and global warps. The highest error rate was 8.08% for a Global warp of 360. A marginal increase (less than 2x) in the error rate is observed when multiple distortions are applied at moderate levels but the error rates still stay low (< 6%). With all error rates less than 10%, it is clear that the NN is very effective at recognizing characters even in the presence of significant distortions.

Table 1. Computer single character recognition error rates for affine transformations and warp. The baseline setting uses 80% - 120% scaling (x-, y-, or both), -20 to +20 degrees of rotation, and a global warp setting of 75.

Distortion (parameter range)	Computer Error Rates
Rotation (-45° to 45°)	0.00%
Global warp (120, 180, 240, 300, 360)	0.04%, 0.29%, 2.40%, 4.81%, 8.08%
Local warp (20, 40, 60, 80)	0.01%, 0.04%, 0.54%, 3.51%
Local warp (20, 40, 60, 80) + Baseline	0.01%, 0.22%, 1.19%, 5.23%

Experiments five through nine investigated single character computer recognition accuracies in the presence of baseline setting with varying degrees of arc clutter. Foreground arcs are rendered in the same color as characters and are designed to join adjacent HIP characters together. Background arcs are rendered in the background color and as such are designed to break up characters into disconnected pieces. Both foreground and background arcs are of constant thickness. Two levels of arc thickness were chosen with thin arcs being 2 pixels wide and thick arcs being 4-5 pixels wide. The combination of thin and thick arcs were chosen to model the thin and thick portions of characters in the Times font. The number of arcs, N_{arcs}, rendered on or around the character was determined by the arc density, D, using:

$$N_{arcs} = ceil \left[WH(D/S)^2 \right] \qquad (1)$$

where W and H are the width and height of the HIP image, respectively. S is the font size and $ceil$ is the ceiling function. Example 8-character HIPs using these distortions and clutter are presented in Section 4.1. One character HIPs were generated with the same margin as in these figures with a 40 pixel x 40 pixel image centered on the character being used for recognition. Single character recognition experiments used a single character rendered on a 90x50 HIP image at font size 30.

Table 2. Computer single character recognition error rates in the presence of clutter. The baseline setting uses 80% - 120% scaling (x-, y-, or both), -20 to +20 degrees of rotation, global warp at 75, and local warp at 20.

Type of Clutter	Arc Density				
	0.5	1.0	1.5	2.0	2.5
Thin Foreground Arcs + Baseline	0.04%	0.19%	0.75%	1.62%	3.07%
Thick Foreground Arcs + Baseline	0.27%	2.08%	6.11%	22.95%	34.04%
Thin Background Arcs + Baseline	0.00%	0.00%	0.01%	0.00%	0.06%
Thick Background Arcs + Baseline	0.01%	0.10%	0.19%	0.47%	1.16%
Thick Non-intersecting Foreground Arcs + Baseline	0.16%	0.29%	0.36%	0.22%	0.30%

Table 3. Sample images with thick foreground and background arcs.

Type of Clutter	Arc Density				
	0.5	1.0	1.5	2.0	2.5
Thick Foreground Arcs + Baseline	M	M	M	M	M
Thick Background Arcs + Baseline	M	M	M	M	M
Thick Non-intersecting Foreground Arcs + Baseline	M	M	M	M	M

Single character neural network recognition results on the test set are presented in Table 2. Interestingly, the neural network does best against thick background arcs and thick non-intersecting foreground arcs with error rates under 0.5%. The neural network also does well in the presence of thin arcs (foreground and background) with error rates staying below 3.1% even when the arc density is as high as 2.5. In the presence of thick arcs, the neural network does well for arc densities up to 1.5, but dramatically deteriorates at higher densities. Table 3 presents examples of input images containing letter 'M' with thick foreground arcs at different arc densities. Images with thick non-intersecting arcs are also presented for reference. When arc density exceeds 1.5 for thick intersecting foreground arcs, significant parts of the character are lost making them unreadable. This explains the dramatic drop in neural network accuracy. These results clearly indicate that the neural network is very effective at recognizing characters even in the presence of significant arc clutter.

4   Human-Friendly HIPs

Human-friendliness of a HIP encompasses both a) the visual appeal and annoyance factor of a HIP, and also b) how well it utilizes the difference in ability between humans and machines at solving segmentation and recognition tasks. As in the case of HIP security, human-friendliness is affected by each of the HIP design choices (Section 2.2) to different degrees. In general, the annoyance factor increases with increasing HIP length. Most online HIPs do not use more than 8 characters. A dictionary of words or a phonetic generator can make it easy for humans to type in the HIP solution as if it were a pseudo-word. Also, phonetic generators may help in reducing transcription and typing errors. Background and foreground textures and colors help blend the HIP image into the web page (or UI) theme and make it appear less intrusive or taxing to the user.

Many of the design choices that make HIPs human-friendly tend to reduce HIP security and vice versa. However, this is not always the case. Some attributes such as colors, textures, and anti-aliasing have negligible effect on security while they can significantly improve appeal. This might be the reason why MSN, Yahoo v2, and Google use two color HIPs (with varying gray levels). Further, human-friendliness can be affected by factors that have no impact on HIP security, such as the display size and color of the HIP image.

4.1   HIP User Studies

Human-friendliness is best studied through user studies with human participants. Three sets of user studies were conducted to understand human abilities in segmenting and recognizing characters in HIPs. The first set described in Section 4.1.1 explores human accuracy under rotation, scaling, local and global warp independently. The baseline combination of parameters with varying local warp levels was also added to the first set. The second and third sets explore human accuracy in the presence of foreground and background arc clutter and are described in Sections 4.1.2 and 4.1.3, respectively. The studies were designed to be run electronically, allowing participants to do the HIP recognition tasks from the comfort of their own offices. To improve efficiency of these user studies, 8-character HIPs were used. Human accuracy was defined as the percentage of characters correctly recognized. For example, for 8 character HIPs, getting on average 7 characters correct would imply an accuracy of 87.5 percent. The interested reader is referred to [18] for further details on these studies.

As in the case of the computer OCR experiments (Section 3.2.2), parameter settings were not limited to only those ranges that are useful for HIP design. Our goal was to understand human abilities across the board from settings where humans get almost 100% correct to those where they get less than 25% correct[4].

---

[4] For an 8-character HIP a 25% single character accuracy means that on average users can read about 2 out of the 8 characters in the HIP.

4.1.1 Human-Friendliness of Distortions

Seventy six users were recruited to participate in the first set of experiments. All were employees at a large software company. Average age of the participants was 35.2 (range of 22-54 years of age), 17 were female, and all but 12 had normal or corrected-to-normal vision. In addition, 42 wore glasses or contacts of some kind. All but six of the participants had at least an undergraduate education. The HIP parameter settings and ranges were the same as in the computer experiments for distortion. Only one HIP was created at each parameter level, and each participant saw that same exact HIP in a predetermined, randomized order. The seven parameters tested in the first user study were plain (or undistorted) text, translated test, rotated text, scaled text, global warping, local warping, and local warping combined with all the previous parameters at baseline settings (i.e., local warp + baseline).

A total of 68 8-character HIPs were presented to each subject. If the HIP was deemed to be unreadable by the participants, they could enter "unreadable" by pressing a button provided on the website for that trial. Each response provided by the participant was recorded. Total time to complete the experiment was approximately 15 minutes. Sample HIPs from these user studies are presented below. The numbers in parentheses indicate the level.

Plain, Translated, Rotated, and Scaled Text: Participants were very accurate at identifying the plain text letters (Figure 11). 73 participants recognized all letters perfectly, while 3 participants missed a single letter. We conjecture that these were transcription errors. The amount of translation was increased in nine steps from 0% to 40% of the character size (Figure 12). Participants had a very high accuracy rate with translated text. The accuracy rate was 99% or above for all levels. We rotated text in ten incremental steps from 0 degrees to 45 degrees (Figure 13). Participants had a very high accuracy rate with rotated text. The accuracy rate was 99% or above for all levels. Scaled text is text that is stretched or compressed in the x-direction as well as in the y-direction. Text was scaled in eleven incremental steps from 0% to ±50%. Participants had a very high accuracy rate with scaled text. The accuracy rate was 98% or above for all levels.

Global warp: Global warp covers the entire eight-character HIP. We increased the amount of global warping in 11 incremental steps from 0 to 390, as shown in Figure 18. Participants had a very high accuracy rate with levels of global warp up to level 270. Accuracy drops off dramatically with more global warp. A One-Way ANOVA shows that accuracy is reliably different for levels of global warp, $F(10,65) = 73.08$, $p < .001$. Post-hoc tests show that the 0-270 levels of global warp are reliably different from the 300-390 levels of global warp at the $p < .05$ level, using Bonferroni corrections for multiple tests in this and all following post-hocs.

Scaling
(20, 35, 50)

Global warp
(180, 270, 360)

Local warp
(30, 55, 80)

Local warp
plus baseline
(30, 80)

Fig. 17. Example of Baseline rotation, translation and scale for studying local warp and arc clutter.

Local warp: The local warp was incremented in 16 steps from 0 to 90, as shown in Figure 19. The local warp value indicates the magnitude of the local warp field and is proportional to the average movement of ink pixels in the HIP. Participants had a very high accuracy rate with levels of local warp up to level 45, and very poor accuracy at level 70 and above. A One-Way ANOVA shows that accuracy is reliably different for local warp levels, $F(15,60) = 120.24$, $p < .001$. Post-hoc tests indicate that levels 0-60 are reliably different from levels 65-90.

Local warp plus baseline: The baseline setting is used and local warp is gradually increased. Participants had a high accuracy rate with local warp plus baseline up to level 55 of local warp, as shown in Figure 20. After level 50, accuracy decreased in gradual steps, as is shown in the figure. A One-Way ANOVA shows that accuracy is reliably different for different levels of local warp plus baseline, $F(15,60) = 98.08$, $p < .001$. Post-hoc tests show that levels 0-55 are reliably different from levels 70-90.

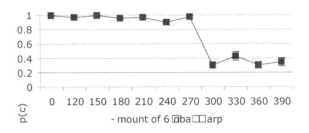

Fig. 18. Accuracy rate for global warp text

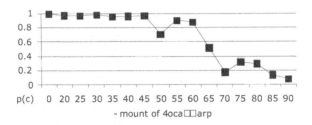

Fig. 19. Accuracy rate for local warp text

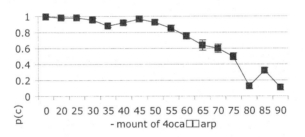

Fig. 20. Accuracy rate for local warp text with baseline

4.1.2 Human-Friendliness of Foreground Clutter

Twenty-nine more users from the same large software company were recruited for the second set of experiments. Average age of the participants was 35.2 (range of 26-54 years of age), 10 were female, and 23/29 had normal or corrected-to-normal vision. In addition, 19 wore glasses or contacts of some kind. All but six of the participants had at least an undergraduate education. Despite the similarities in the profiles between participants in studies 1 and 2, only one participant participated in both studies.

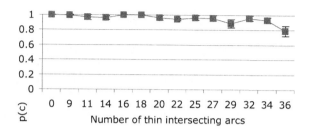

Fig. 21. Accuracy rate for thin intersecting arcs

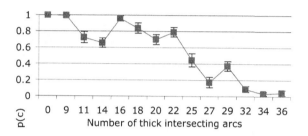

Fig. 22. Accuracy rate for thick intersecting arcs

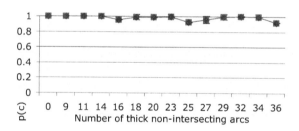

Fig. 23. Accuracy rate for thick non-intersecting arcs

The HIP parameter settings and ranges were similar to the ones in the computer experiments for clutter (Section 3.2.2). Only one HIP was created at each parameter level, and each participant saw that same exact HIP in a predetermined, randomized order. A total of 70 8-character HIPs with different types of arc clutter were presented to each subject. Other than the new HIP examples, all of details of the study were identical to Study 1. Sample HIPs from these user studies are presented in Figure 24.

Thin arcs that intersect plus baseline: There are 14 levels of arcs ranging from 0 to 36 arcs across the HIP, as shown in Figure 21. Participants had a high accuracy rate with thin arcs that intersect plus baseline, with accuracy above 90% for all but the highest number of arcs examined. A One-Way ANOVA shows that accuracy is reliably different for levels of thin arcs that intersect plus baseline, $F(13,16) = 2.70$, $p < .01$. Despite reliable main effects, post-hoc tests found no reliable differences between any two conditions.

Thin arcs that intersect
plus baseline (18, 36)

Thick arcs that intersect
plus baseline (18, 36)

Thick arcs that don't intersect
plus baseline (18,36)

Fig. 24. Sample HIPs from user study 1.

Thick arcs that intersect plus baseline: The baseline setting is combined with 14 levels of thick arcs that cross over the HIP characters, as shown in Figure 22. The number of arcs used ranged from 0 to 36. Not surprisingly, thick arcs that intersect are also difficult for participants when the baseline distortions are also incorporated. A One-Way ANOVA shows that accuracy is reliably different, $F(13,16) = 49.27$, $p < .001$. Post-hoc tests show that levels 0-22 are reliably different from levels 27-36.

Thick arcs that don't intersect plus baseline: The baseline is combined with 14 levels of thick arcs that do not cross over the HIP characters. The number of arcs used ranged from 0 to 36. Participants had a very high accuracy rates of 92% or above for all levels. The differences between levels of arcs was reliably different, $F(13,16) = 2.12$, $p < .05$. Despite the reliable main effect, post-hoc tests did not find any reliable differences between any two conditions (Figure 23).

4.1.3 Human-Friendliness of Background Clutter

Thirty-eight more participants from the same large software company were recruited for the third set of experiments. Average age of the participants was 33.4 (range of 22-57 years of age), nine were female, three were left-handed. All but five of the participants had at least an undergraduate education. Only one participant participated in one of the previous studies (study 2). The HIP parameter settings and ranges were similar to corresponding ones in the computer experiments (Table 3). A total of 12 8-character HIPs with different types of arc clutter were presented to each subject. Other than the new HIP examples, all of details of the study were identical to Studies 1 and 2. Sample HIPs from these studies are presented below

Thin background arcs plus
baseline (27, 45)

Thick background arcs
plus baseline (18, 36)

Fig. 25. Sample HIPs from user study 2.

Thin background arcs with baseline: In this condition, a HIP with the baseline settings is combined with 6 levels of thin background arcs that cross over the HIP characters. As shown in figure 26, background arcs in general break up characters into disjoint pieces. The number of arcs used ranged from 0 to 54. A higher number of background arcs were used as only background arcs that intersect characters show up on the HIP image. Participants had a very high accuracy rate with thin background arcs plus the baseline warp. The accuracy rate was 99% or above for all levels . The differences between the numbers of arcs is not reliably different, $F(5,32) = 1.42$, p > .05.

Thick background arcs with baseline: In this condition, a HIP with the baseline warp settings is combined with 6 levels of thick background arcs that cross over the HIP characters. Character breakup due to background arcs is more noticeable when thick arcs are used. The number of arcs used ranged from 0 to 54, as shown in Figure 27. Participants had a very high accuracy rate with thick background arcs except at the highest setting (54 thick arcs). The accuracy rate was 95% or above for levels up to 27 thick arcs and above 80% for higher levels up to 45. At level 54 the accuracy drops below 25% as characters become unreadable.

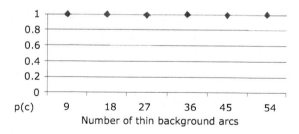

Fig. 26. Accuracy rate for thin background arcs

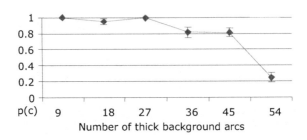

Fig. 27. Accuracy rate for thick background arcs

5   Building Better HIPs

5.1   Lessons Learned

The HIP breaking experiments have shown that many existing HIPs are pure recognition tasks and can be easily broken using machine learning. The stronger HIPs derive their strength from the segmentation part of the HIP challenge they pose, rather than the recognition problem. Recognition of characters in today's HIPs (given correct segmentation) is possible with high accuracy using convolutional neural networks [6].

Computer experiments on single character recognition have shown that neural networks effectively solve the recognition problem even when the distortion levels and clutter densities are driven very high. HIP user studies have shown that human recognition is good under translation, rotation, and scale variations with low to moderate levels of local and global warp. The human ability to solve HIPs is also good in the presence of thin foreground arcs, thick non-intersecting foreground arcs and thin and thick background arcs. However, humans do not do well in the presence of moderate to high levels of thick foreground arcs. Computers do relatively better in handling thick foreground arcs but also deteriorate significantly at high densities.

Comparing computer and human performance, we see that computers are better than humans at recognition (when segmentation is solved). One should note that the user studies (Section 4.1) required humans to solve both the segmentation and recognition problems whereas single character computer recognition experiments (Section 3.2) only required the neural network to solve the recognition problem[5]. In the distortion experiments and at low clutter densities these two results can be directly compared (as segmentation is trivial in these cases). However, at high distortion and clutter densities such a comparison would not be valid. We plan to study these scenarios more directly in future experiments and HIP user studies.

Segmentation is intrinsically difficult for both computers and humans because:

1) Segmentation is computationally expensive. In order to find valid patterns, a recognizer must attempt recognition at many different candidate locations.

---

[5] We do not expect human performance to improve significantly if characters were pre-segmented. This is due to humans being extremely good at segmentation.

2) The segmentation function is complex. To segment successfully, the system must learn to identify which patterns are valid among the set of all possible valid and non-valid patterns. This task is intrinsically more difficult than classification because the space of input is considerably larger. Unlike the space of valid patterns, the space of non-valid patterns is typically too vast to sample. This is a problem for many learning algorithms which yield too many false positives when presented non-valid patterns.

3) Identifying valid characters among a set of valid and invalid candidates is a combinatorial problem. For example, correctly identifying which 8 characters among 20 candidates (assuming 12 false positives), has a 1 in 125,970 (20 choose 8) chances of success by random guessing.

5.2 Segmentation Based HIPs

We can use what we have learned to build better HIPs. The HIP in Figure 28 was designed to make segmentation difficult and a similar version has been deployed by MSN Passport for hotmail registrations.

Fig. 28. Three samples of example segmentation HIP 1 (P6VGA73C, E96U5V9D, N9ZZKNTV).

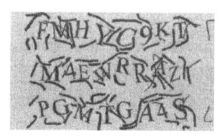

Fig. 29. Three samples of example segmentation HIP 2 (FMHYC9KT, M4EWRRAZ, PGMTGA4S).

The idea is that the additional arcs are themselves good candidates for false characters. The previous segmentation attacks would fail on this HIP. Furthermore, simple changes of fonts, distortions, or arc types would require extensive work for the attacker to adjust to. We believe HIPs that emphasize the segmentation problem, such as the above example, are much stronger than the HIPs we examined in this paper, which rely on recognition being difficult. Pushing this to the extreme, we can easily generate HIPs shown in Figure 29.

Despite the apparent difficulty of these HIPs, humans are surprisingly good at solving them, as suggested by Figure 23, indicating that humans are far better than computers at segmentation (Section 5.3.2 has the details). This approach of adding several competing false positives can in principle be used to strengthen a HIP by posing difficult segmentation problems for hackers.

5.2.1 Segmentation HIP Security

To build an automatic segmentor, we could use the following procedure. Label characters based on their correct position and train a recognizer. Apply the trained recognizer at all locations in the HIP image. Collect all candidate characters identified with high confidence by the recognizer. Compute the probability of each combination of candidates (going from left to right), and output the solution string with the highest probability. This is better illustrated with an example.

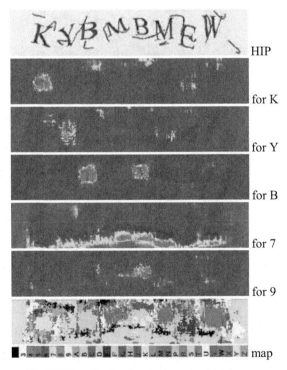

Fig. 30. Neural network output and combined map

Consider the HIP in Figure 30. After training a neural network with the above procedure, we have these maps (warm colors indicate recognition with high confidence) that show that K, Y, and so on are correctly identified. However, the maps for 7 and 9 show several false positives. In general, we would have a map for all the different candidates (see Figure 30).

We note that there are several false positives for each true positive. The number of false positives per true positive character was found to be between 1 and 4, resulting in a 1 in C(16,8) = 12,870 to 1 in C(32,8) = 10,518,300 random chance of guessing the correct segmentation for the HIP characters. These numbers can be improved upon by constraining solution strings to flow sequentially from left to right and by restricting overlap. For each combination, we compute a probability by multiplying the 8 probabilities of the classifier for each position. The combination with the highest probability is proposed by the classifier. We do not have results for such an automatic segmentor at this time. It is interesting to note that with such a method a classifier that is robust to false positives would do far better than one that is not.

5.2.2 Human-Friendliness of Segmentation Based HIPs

One user study was conducted to determine human-friendliness of the segmentation based HIPs presented in figures 28 and 29. The same set of 38 users from section 4.1.3 were used in these experiments. Ten eight-character HIPs of each type were used in the study. Other than the new HIP examples, all of details of the study were identical to the three user studies from Section 4.1. Participants had a very high accuracy rate for both segmentation based HIPs. Accuracy for HIP 1 was above 91% (Figure 28), while accuracy for segmentation HIP 2 was above 89% (Figure 29). Overall accuracy was slightly lower for segmentation HIP 2 examples, but the difference between the two was not statistically reliable, $t(37) = 1.27$, $p = 0.21$. The lack of any statistically significant difference indicates that both of these challenges are of somewhat equal difficulty to humans, though segmentation HIP 2 (Figure 29) poses a much harder segmentation problem for computers.

6 Conclusion

In this paper, we have successfully applied machine learning to investigate HIP security and we studied human reading ability under distortions and clutter common to HIPs. We have learned that decomposing the HIP problem into segmentation and recognition greatly simplifies analysis. Recognition on even unprocessed images (given segmentation is solved) can be done automatically using neural networks. Further, the HIP user studies have shown that given correct segmentation, computers are much better at HIP character recognition than humans. Segmentation, on the other hand, is the difficulty differentiator between weaker and stronger HIPs. Preliminary user studies on segmentation based HIP indicate that humans are just as good at solving segmentation based HIPs as they are at solving recognition based HIPs. In light of these results, we propose that segmentation based reading challenges are the future for building stronger human-friendly HIPs. The contribution of this research is to continue to drive HIP design from a user-centered perspective, wherein we try to design for a "sweet spot" that maximizes the comfort of human solvers while minimizing the ease of the code being broken through machine learning.

Acknowledgements
We would like to acknowledge Chau Luu for her help with developing the website for the user studies. We would also like to acknowledge Cem Paya, Erren Lester, Shannon Kallin, Julien Couvreur and Jonathan Wilkins in the MSN Passport team, for helping with the design, testing, and deployment of new segmentation based human-friendly HIPs. Finally we would like to thank Josh Benaloh from the MSR crypto group for not letting us compromise security.

References

1. Baird HS (1992), "Anatomy of a versatile page reader," *IEEE wroceedings*, v.80, pp. 1059-1065.
2. Chellapilla K, and Simard P, "Using Machine Learning to Break Visual Human Interaction Proofs (HIPs)," NIPS 2004, MIT Press.
3. *First Workshop on Human Interactive wroofs*, Palo Alto, CA, January 2002.
4. Von Ahn L, Blum M, and Langford J, *The (aptcha wro&ct.* http://www.captcha.net
5. Baird HS and Popat K (2002) "Human Interactive Proofs and Document Image Analysis," *wroc. IAw- 2002 Workshop on Document Analysis Systems*, Princeton, NJ.
6. Simard PY, Steinkraus D, and Platt J, (2003) "Best Practice for Convolutional Neural Networks Applied to Visual Document Analysis," in ICDAR'03, pp. 958-962, IEEE Computer Society, Los Alamitos.
7. Mori G and Malik J (2003), "Recognizing Objects in Adversarial Clutter: Breaking a Visual CAPTCHA," CVPR'03, IEEE Computer Society, vol.1, pages:I-134 - I-141, 2003.
8. Chew M and Baird HS (2003), "BaffleText: a Human Interactive Proof," *wroc., 10th ISd TzßwIE Document - ecognition d - etrieval (onf.,* Santa Clara, CA, Jan. 22.
9. LeCun Y, Bottou L, Bengio Y, and Haffner P, "Gradient-based learning applied to document recognition,' *wroceedings of the IEEE*, Nov. 1998.
10. Selfridge OG. (1959). Pandemonium: A paradigm for learning. In *Symposium in the mechanization of thought process* (pp.513-526). London: HM Stationery Office.
11. Pelli DG, Burns CW, Farrell B, and Moore DC, "Identifying letters." (accepted) *"ision - esearch.*
12. Goodman J and Rounthwaite R, "Stopping Outgoing Spam," Proc. of the 5th ACM conf. on Electronic commerce, New York, NY. 2004.
13. Baird HS and Luk M, "Protecting Websites with Reading-Based CAPTCHAs," *Second International Web Document Analysis Workshop* (WDA'03); 2003 August 3; Edinburgh; Scotland.
14. Coates AL, Baird HS, and Fateman RJ, "Pessimal Print: A Reverse Turing Test," *Sixth International (onference on Document Analysis and - ecognition (I(DA- '01),* September 10 - 13, 2001, Seattle, WA.
15. Thayananthan A, Stenger B, Torr PHS, Cipolla R, "Shape Context and Chamfer Matching in Cluttered Scenes," CVPR (1) 2003: 127-133.
16. Moy G, Jones N, Harkless C, Potter R, "Distortion Estimation Techniques in Solving Visual CAPTCHAs," CVPR'04, Volume 2, pp. 23-28, June 27 - July 02, 2004, Washington, D.C., USA.
17. Deriche R, "Fast Algorithms for Low-Level Vision", *IEEE Trans. on wAMI*, 12(1), January 1990, pp. 78-87.
18. Chellapilla K, Larson K, Simard P, and Czerwinski M, "Designing Human Friendly Human Interaction Proofs (HIPs)," in Conference on Human factors In computing systems, CHI 2005. ACM Press.

A Highly Legible CAPTCHA
That Resists Segmentation Attacks

Henry S. Baird, Michael A. Moll, and Sui-Yu Wang

Computer Science & Engineering Dept
Lehigh University
19 Memorial Dr West
Bethlehem, PA 18017 USA
baird@cse.lehigh.edu, {mam7 | syw2}@lehigh.edu
www.cse.lehigh.edu/~baird

Abstract. A CAPTCHA which humans find to be highly legible and which is designed to resist automatic character–segmentation attacks is described. As first detailed in [BR05], these 'ScatterType' challenges are images of machine-print text whose characters have been pseudorandomly cut into pieces which have then been forced to drift apart. This scattering is designed to repel automatic segment-then-recognize computer vision attacks. We report results from an analysis of data from a human legibility trial with 57 volunteers that yielded 4275 CAPTCHA challenges and responses. We have located an operating regime—ranges of the parameters that control cutting and scattering—within which human legibility is high (better than 95% correct) even though the degradations due to scattering remain severe.

Keywords: *CAPTCHAs, human interactive proofs, document image analysis, abuse of web sites and services, human/machine discrimination, Turing tests, OCR performance evaluation, document image degradations, legibility of text, segmentation, fragmentation, Gestalt perception, style-consistent recognition*

1 Introduction

In 1997 Andrei Broder and his colleagues at the DEC Systems Research Center, developed a scheme to block the abusive automatic submission of URLs to the AltaVista web-site [Bro01,LBBB01]. Their approach was to challenge a potential user to read an image of printed text formed specially so that machine vision (OCR) systems could not read it but humans still could. Since that time, inspired also by Alan Turing's 1950 proposal of methods for validating claims of artificial intelligence [Tur50], many such CAPTCHAs—Completely Automated Public Turing tests to tell Computers and Humans Apart—have been developed, including CMU's EZ-Gimpy [BAL00, HB01], PARC's PessimalPrint [CBF01] and BaffleText [CB03], Paypal's CAPTCHA [Pay02], Microsoft's CAPTCHA [SSB03], and Lehigh's ScatterType [BR05]. As discussed more fully in [BR05], fully or partially successful attacks on some of these CAPTCHAs have been reported. We and other CAPTCHA researchers believe that many, perhaps

H.S. Baird and D.P. Lopresti (Eds.): HIP 2005, LNCS 3517, pp. 27–41, 2005.
© Springer-Verlag Berlin Heidelberg 2005

most, CAPTCHAs now in use are vulnerable to (possibly custom-tailored) preprocessing that segments the words into characters, followed by off-the-shelf or slightly
customized OCR. These observations motivated us to investigate CAPTCHAs which
resist character–segmentation attacks. In [BR05] we first described the ScatterType
CAPTCHA, in which each character image is fragmented using horizontal and vertical cuts, then the fragments are forced apart until it is no longer straightforward automatically to reassemble them into characters. Our personal knowledge of the segment-
and-recognize capabilities of commercial OCR machines—as attested by hundreds of
failure cases discussed in [RNN99]—gives us confidence that they pose no threat to
ScatterType today or for the forseeable future. However, this is a conjecture that must
be tested (see the section on Future Work).

We do not apply image degradations such as blurring, thinning, and additive noise
(cf. [Bai02]) so that will not obscure style-specific shape minutiae in the fragments
such as stroke width, serif form, curve shape, which we speculate may account for
the remarkable human legibility of these pervasively damaged images. Experimental
data reported in [BR05] also showed that subjective ratings of difficulty were strongly
(and usefully) correlated with illegibility. Since then we have carried out a systematic
exploration of the legibility of ScatterType as a function of the generating parameters.
The principal new result is the identification of an operating regime within which human
legibility exceeds 95 per cent.

2   Synthesizing ScatterType Challenges

In this section we briefly review the generating parameters (a fuller discussion is in
[BR05]). ScatterType challenges are synthesized by pseudorandomly choosing: (a) a
text-string; (b) a typeface; and (c) cutting and scattering parameters.

The text strings were generated using the pseudorandom variable–length character
n-gram Markov model described in [CB03], and filtered using an English spelling list
to eliminate all but a few English words. In these trials, no word was ever used twice—
even with different subjects—to ensure that mere familiarity with the words would not
affect legibility. The typefaces used were twenty-one FreeType fonts.

Cutting and scattering are applied, separately to each character (more precisely,
to each character's image within its own 'bounding box'). A scaling dimension (the
"base length") is set equal to the height of the shortest character in the alphabet. Image
operations are performed pseudorandomly to each character separately, controlled by
the following parameters.

Cutting Fraction Each character's bounding box image is cut into rectangular blocks
   of size equal to this fraction of the base length. The resulting x & y cut fractions
   are held constant across all characters in the string, but the offset locations of the
   cuts are chosen randomly uniformly independently for each character.
Expansion Fraction Fragments are moved apart by this fraction of base length held
   constant across all characters in the string.
Horizontal Scatter Each row of fragments (resulting from horizontal cutting) is moved
   horizontally by a displacement chosen independently for each row: this displace-

ment, expressed as a fraction of the base length, is distributed normally with a given mean and standard error. Adjacent rows alternate left and right movements.

Vertical Scatter Each fragment within a row (resulting from vertical cutting) is moved vertically by a displacement chosen randomly independently for each fragment: this displacement, expressed as a fraction of the base length, is distributed normally with a given mean and standard error. Adjacent fragments within a row alternate up and down movements.

The resulting images are combined, governed by this final parameter:

Character Separation The images of cut-and-scattered characters are combined (by pixel-wise Boolean OR) into a final text string image by locating them using the original vertical coordinate of the bounding box center, but separating the boxes horizontally by this fraction of the width of the narrower of the two adjacent characters' bounding boxes.

ScatterType Parameter	Range used in Trial
Cut Fraction (both x & y)	0.25-0.40
Expansion Fraction (both x & y)	0.10-0.30
Horizontal Scatter Mean	0.0-0.40
Vertical Scatter Mean	0.0-0.20
Scatter Standard Error (both h & v)	0.50
Character Separation	0.0-0.15

Fig. 1. ScatterType parameter ranges selected for the human legibility trial.

3   Legibility Trial

Students, faculty, and staff in the Lehigh CSE Dept, and researchers at Avaya Labs Research, were invited to attempt to read ScatterType challenges using ordinary browsers, served by a PHP GUI backed by a MySQL database. A snapshot of the challenge page is shown in Figure 2.

After reading the text and typing the text in, subjects rated the "difficulty level" from "Easy" to "Impossible".

4   Experimental Results

A total of 4275 ScatterType challenges were used in the human legibility trial: they are illustrated in Figures 3-5, at three subjective levels of difficulty: "Easy," medium difficulty, and "Impossible."

Human legibility—percentage of challenges correctly read—is summarized in Figure 6. Overall, human legibility averaged 53%, and exceeded 73% for the two easiest levels. Legibility was strongly correlated with subjective difficulty level, falling off monotonically with increasing subjective difficulty (details in [BR05]).

Sorry! Our CAPTCHAs clearly need some more
work! The correct word was "massatle". You thought it
was "maasatle".
You're getting there...only 25 more to go!

Please type the string and select a difficulty level for this image, or logout to terminate your session

freek

Type in the text :   freek

Easy ──▶ Impossible

Log out

Fig. 2. An example of a ScatterType legibility trial challenge page. The Difficulty Level radio buttons (marked 'Easy' to 'Impossible') were colored Blue, Green, Yellow, Orange, and Red. The text at the top of the page refers to the previously answered challenge.

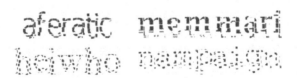

Fig. 3. ScatterType challenges rated by subjects as "Easy" (difficulty level 1 out of 5). All of these examples were read correctly: "aferatic," "memari," "heiwho," "nampaign."

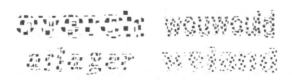

Fig. 4. ScatterType challenges rated by subjects as being of medium difficulty (difficulty level 3 out of 5). Only one of these examples was read correctly (correct/attempt): "ovorch"/"overch", "wouwould", "adager"/"atlager", "weland"/"wejund".

Fig. 5.   ScatterType challenges rated by subjects as "Impossible" (difficulty level 5 out of 5). None of these examples were read correctly (correct/attempt): "echaeva"/"acchown", "gealthas"/"gualing", "beadave"/"bothere", "engaberse"/"caquired"

		Difficulty Level				
	ALL	1	2	3	4	5
Total challenges	4275	610	1056	1105	962	542
% correct answers	52.6	81.3	73.5	56.0	32.8	7.7

Fig. 6. Human reading performance as a function of the difficulty level that the subject selected.

5   A Highly Legible Regime

We have systematically explored the improvements in legibility that can be expected from judicious choices of generating parameters (distributions that control cutting and scattering). We began our project with 4275 ScatterType challenges collected in the human legibility trial. The overall legibility of that set (the fractions of challenges read and typed correctly) was 53%.

We used Tin Kam Ho's Mirage (http://cm.bell-labs.com/who/tkh/mirage/index.html) data analysis tool. For each challenge, we loaded the generation input parameters, the typeface used, the true word, the word guessed by user, the time taken by user to enter the guess, and the user's rating of subjective difficulty. We examined histograms and scatter plots (colorcoded by subjective difficulty if read correctly, with black indicating a mistake) of many single and paired features, looking for strong correlations with either objective or subjective difficulty.

One of the first features examined was the cutting fraction (set equal in both x and y directions), which had been coarsely discretized as either 0.25, 0.32, or 0.40. The cutting fraction determines the size of the rectangular blocks each of the characters bounding boxes are cut into. Therefore a smaller cutting fraction will result in more cuts and more boxes which would seem to imply the smaller the cut fraction, the more difficult the challenge should be to read. We created a Mirage histogram (Figure 7) with the vertical cut fraction on the X axis: our hypothesis was confirmed since for the three distributions of vertical cut fraction 0.25 was the only one to have more illegible than legible samples.

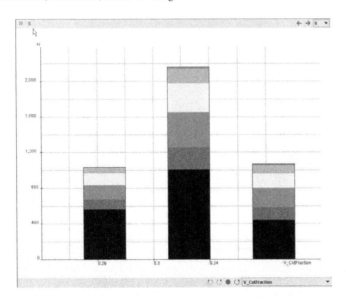

Fig. 7. Mirage histogram of difficulty levels (black marks mistakes) as a function of the CutFraction parameter. The value 0.25 was the only one to have more illegible than legible samples. Black indicates a reading mistake: for legible samples, the colors red, orange, yellow, green, and blue indicate five subjective difficulty levels from "impossible" to "easy".

We then created a scatter plot (Figure 8) with the mean horizontal scatter distance on the x-axis and the mean vertical scatter distance on the y-axis. These features determine how far each row of fragments (as created by the cutting fraction described above) is displaced. The overall displacement is a positive random number that is distributed normally with a mean and standard error. In this experiment we are considering just the means which range between 0.0 and 0.40 horizontally and 0.0 and 0.20 vertically. The scatter plot in Mirage strongly indicates a higher concentration of legible challenges in the lower left hand part of the graph near the origin. Without normalizing the scales, we initially estimate best performance would result by classifying all instances within an Euclidean distance of 0.25 from the origin as legible.

Further exploration did not reveal any other features or pairs of features with strong correlation (positive or negative) to legibility. Two other features that we examined closely (though not within Mirage) are the font and character sets. As shown in an earlier analysis [BR05], four fonts perform significantly worse than the rest, and some characters were confused more frequently than others. The first step we took toward locating a high-legibility regime was to limit the mean scatter distances (since those parameters appeared to show the strongest correlation to legibility in our analysis using Mirage). Consider parameter d, the Euclidean distance of an instance from the origin of the scatter plot (Figure 8) of mean horizontal scatter distance versus mean vertical

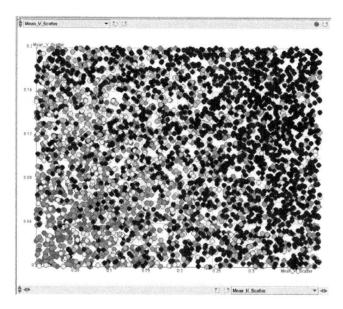

Fig. 8. Mirage scatter plot of the Mean Horizontal Scatter (X-axis) versus Mean Vertical Scatter (Y-axis) parameters. Legible samples clustered strongly near the (0,0) origin. Black indicates a reading mistake: for legible samples, the colors red, orange, yellow, green, and blue indicate five subjective difficulty levels from "impossible" to "easy".

scatter distance. Our initial estimate of setting $d < 0.25$ resulted in a 25% increase (Figure 9), while still correctly classifying over one quarter of the challenges.

We then removed all cut fraction values equal to 0.25 for the reasons described above. These results, however, sharply reduced the set of challenges classified while improving legibility only slightly (Figure 7). However the evidence of worsening performance when it was equal to 0.25 convinced us to omit this value of the parameter. Our next step was to begin removing fonts and characters that did not perform well in the trial. However, the analysis of font pruning in [BR05] showed that removing the four worst fonts resulted in positive but insignificant increases in performance at all subjective difficulty levels, especially for the two easiest levels. We repeated the analysis of removing fonts, in combination with the reduction of the cut fraction and scatter distances and verified that it did not have any correlation to improving legibility (Figure 9). Thus we guessed that pruning fonts was unlikely to help. (Later, after pruning the worst performing characters, this hunch proved correct: pruning fonts in addition caused a *loss* of legibility of four per cent.)

In the preliminary analysis in [BR05], removing the five characters with the highest "confusability"('q', 'c', 'i', 'o', and 'u') brought us rapidly to above 90%. Combined with our new restrictions, we achieved a legibility close to 93% (Figure 9).

From this analysis we concluded that restricting mean scatter distances and pruning the worst performing characters both are strongly positively correlated with legibility, while using larger cut fraction can be somewhat useful when combined with other policies. Removing poorly performing fonts however seem to offer little benefit in increasing legibility (at least in our "simpler" parameter space).

We continued to experiment with features to see if it would be possible to drive the legibility any higher. First we removed the next 3 worst performing characters ('z', 'j' and 'h') and set $d < 0.15$ and removed cut fractions = 0.25 and increased legibility to 94.26% for 115 instances. Removing the next three most confused characters ('f', 'n' and 'l') improved legibility to 95.00%, but for only 38 instances.

Taking another approach, we return to the original 5 characters removed and instead continue to decrease the d threshold to 0.1 and manage to increase legibility even further, and for more correctly classified instances than above, reaching legibility of 97.5

Obviously, a more systematic and careful study of the confusability of characters is necessary to determine which have the greatest detrimental effect on legibility, but we have shown that through removing a small subset of easily confusable characters and manipulating the values two parameters from the original trials, legibility could be raised with confidence to above 95%.

d	Cut Fraction	Fonts Removed	Chars Removed	Legibility	Correct Instances
< 0.25	0.25 - 0.40	None	None	0.697	1656
< 0.20	0.25 - 0.40	None	None	0.755	1309
< 0.15	0.25 - 0.40	None	None	0.815	809
< 0.25	0.32 - 0.40	None	None	0.715	1278
< 0.20	0.32 - 0.40	None	None	0.761	1001
< 0.15	0.32 - 0.40	None	None	0.814	613
< 0.25	0.32 - 0.40	4 Worst	None	0.744	1074
< 0.20	0.32 - 0.40	4 Worst	None	0.780	893
< 0.15	0.32 - 0.40	4 Worst	None	0.813	503
< 0.25	0.32 - 0.40	None	Q, C, I, O, U	0.788	305
< 0.20	0.32 - 0.40	None	Q, C, I, O, U	0.840	226
< 0.15	0.32 - 0.40	None	Q, C, I, O, U	0.929	143
< 0.10	0.32 - 0.40	None	Q, C, I, O, U	0.975	78

Fig. 9. Parameter ranges used to locate a high-legibility regime. d = Euclidean distance of an instance from origin of plot of mean horizontal scatter distance versus mean vertical scatter distance.

6   A Negative Result on Image Complexity

We also investigated one way to construct classifiers for legibility in spaces determined by features that can be extracted from the images of the challenges *after* they are generated. We tested the 'Perimetric Image Complexity' metric that has been reported to be correlated negatively with legibility in the BaffleText trial [CB02]. But, as we will briefly report, this image metric failed to predict illegibility of ScatterType challenges.

Perimetric Image Complexity is an easily computed feature of any bilevel (black and white) image, as the ratio of the square of the perimeter over the black area, where the perimeter is the length of the black/white boundary in pixels. High values correlate positively with fragmentation. In ScatterType we observed many cases where a word image was cut into a great number of pieces and yet remained legible. These cases were numerous enough to vitiate the utility of this metric to predict legibility.

7   Generating New Trials

A first step toward conducting another experiment on the human legibility of these images is to generate new trials with a parameter space constrained by our findings from the first experiment. Words containing the five most confused characters from the first trial were removed and the range for the cut fraction was reduced to 0.32 to 0.40. This was done because the smaller the cut fraction, the more blocks each character is cut into, and in the first experiments this corresponded to increasing difficulty. Also, all parameters that had been coarsely discretized in the first experiment were now more finely distributed (the number of levels for each parameters was increased to 100).

We first attempted to create trials of four different complexity levels, differentiated solely by the scatter distances. This created four classes of trials, labeled as too hard, hard, medium and easy. Upon inspecting the images generated from these parameters, a clear, incremental increase in difficulty was obvious across all four classes, however all of the classes seemed uniformly more difficult than anticipated. The easy class was expected to be almost trivial to read, yet from simply looking at those trials, it was obvious we would have to be very optimistic to expect the legibility of those trials to be over 90

Realizing that simply limiting the scatter distances from the original experiment was simply not enough to raise legibility as high as we hoped, we experimented with creating two more simpler classes, labeled as simple and trivial, by altering the parameters for expansion fraction and cut fraction. In general, the larger the cut fraction becomes, the fewer cuts that are placed in the character, and this should typically result in more legible images, as long as the expansion fraction is also not too large. As expected, the resulting class labeled simple was much easier to read, primarily because of fewer cuts being made to the character, and the class labeled trivial, was very near to the original plain text.

8   Discussion of Sample Images

The following six images illustrate the six subranges of parameters that we chose after analysis of the first experiment. We have named these classes "trivial" (Figure 10), "simple" (Figure 11), easy (Figure 12), "medium hard" (Figure 13), "hard" (Figure 14) and "too hard" (Figure 15). These names are to some extent arbitrary, but they capture our intuition about legibility within each subrange. This is a step towards understanding the ScatterType parameter space well enough to allow us to generate challenges in real time possessing a specified difficulty. In the following six examples, the true word is "telghby" and the font is Courier New Bold.

Fig. 10. A "Trivial" example, generated using a large cut fraction, a small expansion fraction, and no overlap due to the character separation parameter. It is indeed highly legible, so much so that some human readers might not suspect that it was a test of skill.

Fig. 11. A "Simple" example, generated with a cut fraction value that allows roughly two or three cuts and a slightly larger expansion fraction than "trivial" cases. The characters are also slightly less separated.

Fig. 12. An "Easy" example, generated with an expansion fraction greater than for "simple" cases: but it is still easy to segment characters using vertical strokes within wide white space channels. Note that the base of the letter 'h' is starting to merge so that it begins to resemble the letter 'b': but we believe that for most readers it will be obvious that they remain distinct characters.

As these Figures illustrate, from case to case there is a gradual but perceptible increase in difficulty of these images. One potential problem with all six of these particular examples is that it does not seem difficult to segment the characters using vertical cuts in large white spaces: of course this could make them more vulnerable to attack, regardless of the degradation of the individual characters.

We have also selected examples that illustrate instructive and problematic aspects of our approach: we discuss them below.

Fig. 13. A "Medium Hard" example, generated using nearly the same parameters as in the "easy" cases. The principal change is an increase in the scatter distance, which in this example degrades legibility noticeably compared to Figure 12.

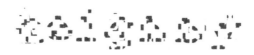

Fig. 14. A "Hard" example, generated using the same parameters as "medium hard" cases, except that scatter distance has been increased. The letter 't' that starts the word is now nearly obliterated. We can still distinguish 'h' from 'b' but it is now difficult to tell which is which.

Fig. 15. A "Too Hard" example, generated using an even larger scatter distance than for the "hard" cases. At this level of difficulty, words often become illegible. Note that the letter 'b' no longer seems to have an appropriate height.

Fig. 16. The correct word is "wexped". This image has been generated using "easy" parameters but it's not highly legible. The cause appears to be small character separation, especially between 'e','x' and 'p'. Without knowing the word, it seems difficult to recover the 'x'. This illustrates the difficulty of achieving 100% legibility within the current ScatterType parameter space.

Fig. 17. The correct word is "veral". As in Figure 16 above, it has been scattered using "easy" parameters, but in a different font. Despite small character separation it isn't as difficult to segment as the prior example. This illustrates the problematic fact that font choice can dominate the effects of the scattering parameters, and in a manner that is hard to predict.

Fig. 18. The correct word is "tpassed". This also was generated using "easy" parameters. It's interesting to see two 's' characters treated so differently within the same word.

Fig. 19. The correct word is "spental". This was also generated using "easy" parameters, but this case happens to achieve the desirable characteristic of being difficult to segment into characters. However, it is potentially ambiguous in its last three letters.

Fig. 20. The correct word is "neved". It is generated using "easy" parameters, but characters are easier to segment than the case in Figure 19. Note that each 'e' is rendered quite differently, and 'n' seems implausibly "mirrored."

Fig. 21. The correct word is "mempear". Generated using easy parameters, it is difficult to segment, but not because of small or negative character separation. Here, it's due to large expansion fraction and scatter distance operating within each character.

Fig. 22. The correct word is "wested". Generated using "medium hard" parameters, the larger scatter distance nearly destroys the legibility of the 's'. Even small increases in parameters can have large effects.

Fig. 23. The correct word is "travame". It was generated using only "medium hard" parameters however, due to interactions with the chosen font, it is uncommonly difficult to read (and to segment). This is another illustration of the interactions between scatter parameters and font which are difficult to predict and control.

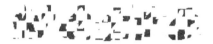

Fig. 24. The correct word is "wezre". Generated using "too hard" parameters, it is for the most part satisfactorily illegible. However it would not perhaps be difficult to segment.

Fig. 25. The correct word is "thern". Generated using "too hard" parameters, it is indeed difficult to read, but easier than most other words generated with same parameters. Even in the more difficult regions of the parameter space, the font chosen can make a large difference in legibility.

After generating 100 sample images for each class and viewing them, we are convinced that it will be necessary to give more careful consideration to the role that font choice plays in legibility. After the first experiment, we concluded that the effect that the worst performing fonts had was greatest on those images generated with the highest subjective difficulty and for the more legible trials, the choice of font did not play as large a part in determining subjective difficulty. While this still appears to hold, it is not obvious that the least confused fonts actually do enhance legibility across all classes of parameters used, as seen in (Figure 15), where using a subjectively easy font makes a word generated with the "too hard" parameters almost legible.

We have seen a great deal of evidence that ScatterType is capable of generating cases where automatic segmentation into characters would be highly problematic, while the images remain legible. This desirable property is the result of two factors: small or negative character separation of course, but also importantly large scatter distances and expansion fractions. By judicious choice of parameters we now believe we can generate a high fraction of cases with this property, but we do not yet fully understand how to guarantee it in all cases.

9   Discussion and Future Work

A systematic analysis of the first ScatterType human legibility trial data has identified an operating regime—a combination of restrictions placed on generating parameters and pruning of the character set—which achieves legibility better than 95%. Within that regime we can pseudorandomly generate many millions of distinct ScatterType challenges. But the correlation of the generating parameters with these desirable properties is weak and we have nearly exhausted our experimental data in locating this regime. Future work to refine the characterization of this regime must await future legibility trials, if only to replenish the data set.

We also hope to investigate a related question: how well can we automatically select those that are likely to possess a given subjective difficulty level?

The fact that ScatterType amplifies certain character-pair confusions and not others in an idiosyncratic way might be exploitable. If further study reveals that the distribution of mistakes differ between human readers and machine vision systems, we may be able to craft policies that forgive the mistakes that humans are prone to while red-flagging machine mistakes.

One reviewer suggested that the Gestalt laws of continuity (of, *e.g.*, straight and curved lines perceived as continuos inspite of breaks) may go far to explain the point of collapse of legibility. This deserves careful analysis.

Another reviewer suggested that since certain characters (*e.g.* 'c', 'e', and 'o') are more vulnerable to ScatterType degradations, they should be generated with restricted range of parameters. This technique might alleviate the problem of generating a sufficient number of nonsense words within a pruned alphabet.

Of course every CAPTCHA including ScatterType must be tested systematically using the best available OCR engines, and should be offered to the research community for attack by experimental machine vision methods.

10   Acknowledgments

We are grateful especially to Terry Riopka, who implemented the first version of ScatterType and ran its first human legibility trial.

We are also grateful for privately communicated observations by Patrice Simard and for illuminating suggestions by Dan Lopresti, Jarret Raim, and Jon Bentley. Also, our experiments have benefited from systems software assistance by Jarret Raim, Bryan Hodgson, and David Morissette.

Above all, we warmly thank the nearly 60 people—students, faculty and staff in the Computer Science & Engineering Dept of Lehigh University, and technical staff at Avaya Labs Research—for volunteering their time for the legibility trial.

References

[BAL00] M. Blum, L. A. von Ahn, and J. Langford, *The CAPTCHA Project*, "Completely Automatic Public Turing Test to tell Computers and Humans Apart," Dept. of Computer Science, Carnegie-Mellon Univ., www.captcha.net, and personal communications, November, 2000.

[BK02] H. S. Baird and K. Popat, "Human Interactive Proofs and Document Image Analysis," *Proc., 5th IAPR Int'l Workshop on Document Analysis Systems*, Princeton, NJ, Springer-Verlag (Berlin) LNCS 2423, pp. 507–518, August 2002.

[BR05] H. S. Baird and T. Riopka, "ScatterType: a Reading CAPTCHA Resistant to Segmentation Attack," *Proc., IS&T/SPIE Document Recognition & Retrieval XII Conf.,*, San Jose, CA, January 16–20, 2005.

[Bro01] AltaVista's "Add-URL" site: altavista.com/sites/addurl/newurl, protected by the earliest known CAPTCHA.

[CB03] M. Chew and H. S. Baird, "BaffleText: a Human Interactive Proof," Proc., 10th SPIE/IS&T Document Recognition and Retrieval Conf. (DRR2003), Santa Clara, CA, January 23–24, 2003.

[CBF01] A. L. Coates, H. S. Baird, and R. Fateman, "Pessimal Print: a Reverse Turing Test," Proc., IAPR 6th Intl. Conf. on Document Analysis and Recognition, Seattle, WA, September 10-13, 2001, pp. 1154-1158.

[HB01] N. J. Hopper and M. Blum, "Secure Human Identification Protocols," In: C. Boyd (Ed.) Advances in Crypotology, Proceedings of Asiacrypt 2001, LNCS 2248, pp.52 -66, Springer-Verlag Berlin, 2001

[LABB01] M. D. Lillibridge, M. Abadi, K. Bharat, and A. Z. Broder, "Method for Selectively Restricting Access to Computer Systems," U.S. Patent No. 6,195,698, Issued February 27, 2001.

[LPRS85] G. E. Legge, D. G. Pelli, G. S. Rubin, & M. M. Schleske, "Psychophysics of Reading: I. Normal Vision," *Vision Research*, Vol. 25, No. 2, pp. 239–252, 1985.

[MM03] G. Mori and J. Malik, "Recognizing Objects in Adversarial Clutter: Breaking a Visual CAPTCHA," Proc., IEEE CS Society Conf. on Computer Vision and Pattern Recognition (CVPR'03), Madison, WI, June 16-22, 2003.

[NS96] G. Nagy and S. Seth, "Modern optical character recognition." in *The Froehlich / Kent Encyclopaedia of Telecommunications*, Vol. 11, pp. 473-531, Marcel Dekker, NY, 1996.

[Pav00] T. Pavlidis, "Thirty Years at the Pattern Recognition Front," King-Sun Fu Prize Lecture, 11th ICPR, Barcelona, September, 2000.

[Pay02] PayPal Captha, on display starting in 2002 at www.paypal.com.

[RNN99] S. V. Rice, G. Nagy, and T. A. Nartker, *OCR: An Illustrated Guide to the Frontier*, Kluwer Academic Publishers, 1999.

[RJN96] S. V. Rice, F. R. Jenkins, and T. A. Nartker, "The Fifth Annual Test of OCR Accuracy," ISRI TR-96-01, Univ. of Nevada, Las Vegas, 1996.

[SCA00] A. P. Saygin, I. Cicekli, and V. Akman, "Turing Test: 50 Years Later," *Minds and Machines*, 10(4), Kluwer, 2000.

[SN05] P. Sarkar & G. Nagy, "Style Consistent Classification of Isogenous Patterns," *IEEE Trans. on PAMI*, Vol. 27, No. 1, January 2005.

[SSB03] P. Y. Simard, R. Szeliski, J. Benaloh, J. Couvreur, I. Calinov, "Using Character Recognition and Segmentation to Tell Computer from Humans," Proc., IAPR Int'l Conf. on Document Analysis and Recognition, Edinburgh, Scotland, August 4–6, 2003.

[Tur50] A. Turing, "Computing Machinery and Intelligence," *Mind*, Vol. 59(236), pp. 433–460, 1950.

[VN05] S. Veeramachaneni & G. Nagy, "Style context with second order statistics," *IEEE Trans. on PAMI*, Vol. 27, No. 1, January 2005.

Visual CAPTCHA with Handwritten Image Analysis*

Amalia Rusu and Venu Govindaraju

Center of Excellence for Document Analysis and Recognition (CEDAR)
Department of Computer Science and Engineering, University at Buffalo
Buffalo, NY, USA
{air2, govind}@cedar.buffalo.edu

Abstract. By convention, CAPTCHA is an automated test that humans can pass but current computer programs can't. In general, the research on CAPTCHA and Human Interactive Proofs is focusing on those recognition tasks that are harder for machines than for humans. The recognition of unconstrained handwriting continues to be a difficult task for computers and handwritten image analysis is still an unsolved problem. Therefore, handwriting recognition provides a reasonable gap between humans and machines that could be exploited and used for new CAPTCHA challenges. In this paper we use handwritten word images and explore Gestalt psychology to motivate our image transformations. The deformation methods are individually described and results are presented and compared to other traditional handwritten image transformations. Several applications for Web services would find our handwritten CAPTCHA an excellent biometric for online security and a way of defending online services against abusive attacks.

1 Introduction

If you tried to get an email account with Yahoo or Hotmail you may have seen a registration check in the form of an image, like a puzzle that needs to be deciphered in order to register for a free account. The reason for this is that typing the characters from an image helps ensure that a person, not an automated program, is completing the registration form. Currently this is an important issue for online services due to increasing number of malicious programs that try to register for a large number of free accounts using Internet services and then use these accounts to cause problems for other users. Possible problems that they may cause are sending junk e-mail messages or slowing down the service by repeatedly signing in to multiple accounts simultaneously or causing denial of services. In most cases, an automated registration computer program does not recognize the characters in the image whereas humans should not have any problem.

Now, how to prove that you are a human and not an automated computer program over the Internet? The idea of proving humanity is not a new one. It

---

* Research supported in part by Calspan-UB Research Center, Buffalo, NY.

H.S. Baird and D.P. Lopresti (Eds.): HIP 2005, LNCS 3517, pp. 42–52, 2005.

is another formulation of Alan Turing's old question: "Can machine think?". In 1950 Turing proposed a way of testing whether machines can think through experiments that involve interrogation on both human and computer and the interrogator should be able to distinguish them accordingly [19]. In order to make use of this concept for our purpose, a new formulation was defined and the changes are that the interrogation is conducted by the computer and it is also the grader. We name the tests administrated automatically by machines – CAPTCHA (Completely Automatic Public Turing tests to tell Computers and Humans Apart).

Looking for ways to distinguish between humans and computers, we have found that the most trivial task that could differentiate them is handwriting recognition. Understanding handwritten words is a common activity that humans perform effortlessly. However, making a computer to perform the same task involves techniques from several areas, including pattern recognition, image processing, computer vision, artificial intelligence, language understanding, and psychology. As of now, handwriting recognition continues to be a challenge for computers even that is the most common task for humans.

In this paper we describe how image analysis in general and handwritten text images in particular could serve as challenges for machine and be used as valid CAPTCHA puzzles. In our previous work we identified the problems with a couple of machine printed text CAPTCHAs that have been already broken and established handwritten word recognition as a better candidate for CAPTCHA. We now wish to enrich our previous experiments and add a new point of view that has proven to play an important role in handwriting recognition. Specifically, we will make use of Gestalt Philosophy and use the perception laws to create more sophisticated yet automatically image challenges. Our focus is on automatic generation of CAPTCHA challenges (Fig. 1). Holistic features [12] are investigated since they are widely believed to be inspired by psychological studies of human reading.

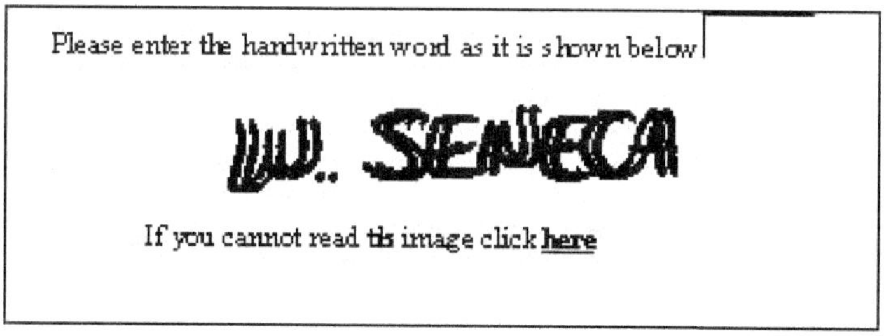

Fig. 1. Example of interface and handwritten CAPTCHA to confirm registration

2   Previous Work

The first known CAPTCHA was introduced on the AltaVista website to block the abusive automatic submission of URLs [1]. Similar ideas and research efforts on HIPs and CAPTCHAs have been made at the Carnegie Mellon University, PARC and UC Berkeley either by creating CAPTCHAs or tools to break them through [2,3,4,5,6,7,13,20]. So far, the CAPTCHAs currently in use take advantage of superior human ability in reading machine printed text, as well as using speech and facial recognition [10,15]. Several current machine printed text based CAPTCHAs have been already broken: Greg Mori and Jitendra Malik of the UCB have written a program that can solve Ez-Gimpy with accuracy 83%; Thayananthan, Stenger, Torr, and Cipolla of the Cambridge vision group have written a program that can achieve 93% correct recognition rate against Ez-Gimpy, and Gabriel Moy, Nathan Jones, Curt Harkless, and Randy Potter of Arete Associates have written a program that can achieve 78% accuracy against Gimpy-R [5].

In this paper, we present handwritten word CAPTCHA that exploits the gap between human and machine recognition of handwritten text. Handwritten text offers challenges that are rarely encountered in machine-printed text. In addition, most problems faced in reading machine-printed text, for example character recognition, word segmentation, or letter segmentation, are more severe in handwritten text. Intuitively, the current sources of OCR errors lead to the conclusion that handwritten word recognition would be the best candidate for CAPTCHA for years to come. Our paper continues the effort in conducting research on CAPTCHA using handwritten text challenges [16,17].

3   Technical Approach

The goal is to motivate our approach for creating the handwritten CAPTCHAs from the cognitive point of view. We will make use of the features in the visual world and the laws that administrate it. A general feature extractor for handwritten characters and words identifies for example the strokes (vertical, horizontal), aspect ratio, holes, arcs, cross points, concavities, convexities etc. By altering the characters and words we modify the feature mapping function in the parametric space and try to eliminate or add features that otherwise map closely together or break them apart in the parameter space for the characters in the same or different class.

While in the past we focused on distortions and transformations that may work in general for any type of images, in our current work we extend the research on more elaborated techniques, underlining the inefficiency of handwritten word recognition by machines in certain cases. In particular, we are interested to analyze the recognition behavior when considering the holistic aspects used in human reading. A good starting point to consider is the relationship with Gestalt psychology.

Gestalt psychology is based on the observation that we often experience things that are not part of our simple sensations. What we are seeing is believed to be an effect of the whole event, and not contained in the sum of the parts. This concept resembles the holistic approaches that focus on recognizing the entire word.

In perception, there are many organizing principles called *gestalt laws* [11]. They include the laws of closure, similarity, proximity, symmetry, continuity, familiarity and figure-ground distinction (Fig. 2). Humans are amazing in perceiving the object of interest: we tend to complete a figure in the way it should be, if something is missing in an otherwise complete figure we will tend to close it, fill the gap, we tend to group similar items together to see if there could form a larger object, we imagine things that are close together as belonging together etc. These laws are not restricted to perception only, it is just where they were first noticed. An example of this kind is memory. For example, if you see an irregular figure, it is likely that your memory will straighten it out for you a bit. Or if you experience something that does not quite make sense you will tend to remember it as having meaning that may not have been there. Also, internal metric relations play a role as part of an outside iconic memory.

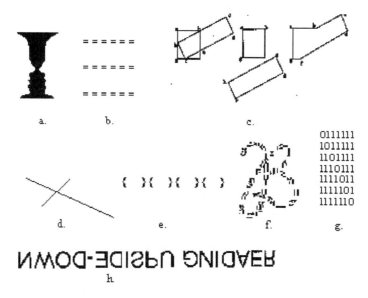

Fig. 2. Image analysis with gestalt laws as described by Gestalt Psychology of Kurt Koffka. Common examples for *figure-ground* (a), *proximity* (b), *familiarity* (c), *continuity* (d), *symmetry* (e), *closure* (f), *similarity* (g), and *memory* (h)

In contrast to human perception, currently the machines have no such abilities (yet). Our task is to remove features or add non-textual strokes or noise to a handwritten image in a systematic fashion based on Gestalt segmentation and grouping principles in order to break machine recognition but preserve overall

letter legibility and word recognition from features for humans. We started by
taking every law and applying it on handwritten strokes. We have found that
every law in particular could be translated into several methods that could be
used as valuable transformations on handwritten images. We used the following
set of candidate transforms to mimic these laws and tested them on handwritten
images:

Method 1: Create horizontal or vertical overlaps: for same words smaller dis-
tance overlaps, for different words bigger distance overlaps.
Gestalt laws: Law of proximity, symmetry, familiarity, continuity, background
(Fig. 3).

Fig. 3. Examples of handwritten images where OCR systems fail. The truth
words are: *Silver Creek, New York, Lockport, Young America* and *W.Seneca*

Method 2: Add occlusions by circles, rectangles, lines with random angles.
Gestalt laws: Law of closure, proximity, continuity (Fig. 4).

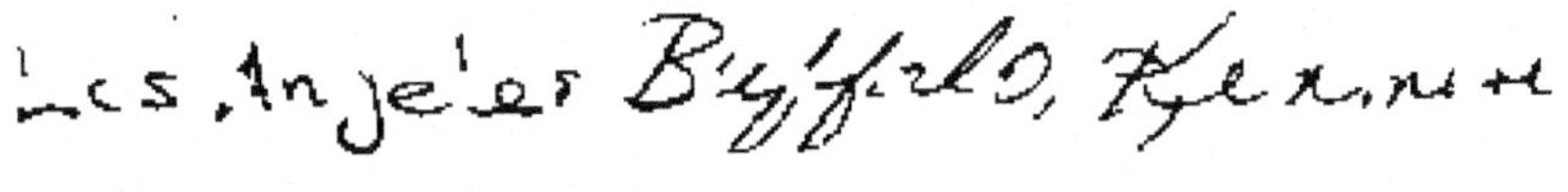

Fig. 4. Examples of handwritten images where OCR systems fail. The truth
words are: *Los Angeles, Buffalo, Kenmore*

Method 3: Add occlusions by waves (or thick lines) from left to right on entire
image, with various amplitudes or wavelength or rotate them by an angle.
Gestalt laws: Law of closure, proximity, continuity (Fig. 5).

Fig. 5. Examples of handwritten images where OCR systems fail. The truth
words are: *Young America, Clinton, Blasdell*

Method 4: Add occlusion using the same pixels as the foreground pixels (black
pixels), arcs, or lines.
Gestalt laws: Law of familiarity, background (Fig. 6).

Fig. 6. Examples of handwritten images where OCR systems fail. The truth words are: *Rockport, Albany, Buffalo*

Method 5: Change word orientation entirely, or the orientation for few letters only.

Gestalt laws: Memory, internal metrics, familiarity of letters and letter orientation (Fig. 7).

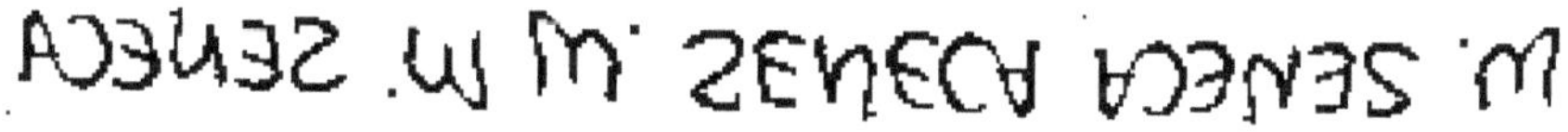

ΛƆƷЧƷᄅ .ᴜ ᴍⁱ ᄅƐИƐƆᴧ ᴆƆƷИƷƧ ⁱᴍ

Fig. 7. Examples of handwritten images where OCR systems fail. Horizontal mirror, vertical mirror, flip-flop. The truth words is: *W.Seneca*

We need to mention that all the methods described here would clearly work for machine-printed text images, the same as the other methods described so far in literature for machine-printed text images would work for handwritten text images. However, the advantage of using handwriting is that most handwritten text challenges are uniquely problematic and usually more severe than problems encountered in recognizing machine-printed text. By using handwriting we are adding more difficulties to the machine recognition task but we do not alter the human recognition capabilities in any way since handwriting recognition is the most common task for humans. To match human performance in machine recognition of handwritten characters and words is not a straightforward task. On the contrary, people can recognize characters of different sizes and rotations, either handwritten or machine printed, by the time they are five years old, and they maintain the same high performance level of recognition for confusing or distorted handwritten text [14].

4   Testing Results

For our experiments, we used the two most advanced word recognizers available at CEDAR: Word Model Recognizer (WMR) and Accuscript (HMM) [8,9,22]. Both recognizers use static lexicons in the recognition process. We applied transformations on a set of about 4,100 handwritten city name images. We created several new sets of transformed images, one set for each transformation previously described. We randomly chose some parameters values for our transformations and successively applied them on our handwritten test images. While trying to make recognition harder by using various image transformations, we still work under the assumption that a valid lexicon is provided and that it comprises all of the city names that we use in our tests.

We performed a series of tests by varying some parameters such as in the case of first method where we tried for various displacements of overlap on vertical and horizontal direction. We noticed that by increasing the displacement on horizontal the error rate for machines increases but it also poses problems for humans since visual segmentation becomes misleading as shown in Fig. 8.

Fig. 8. Original city name is *Williamsville*. If we increase the displacement too much, then it becomes *Wiilllliiamsvillllee*

The accuracy achieved by handwriting recognizers is presented in Table 1. The last method that illustrates the flip-flop transform was not tested due to the nature of our recognizers, as well as the overlap of two different handwritten words. Clearly the accuracy for these cases would be 0 if using our test recognizers, but we do not count these results yet since our current recognizers are not trained for this kind of images. The most efficient methods based on our results are duplicating the word on vertical or adding black occlusions such as waves, lines, arcs. While computers have major difficulties in recognizing them, humans have the least troubles with this kind of images. The gestalt law of differentiating between background and foreground holds in this case, and humans easily continue the characters that are overlapped and eliminate the background noise.

Table 1. The accuracy of handwriting recognizers for current image transformations

Transformation	WMR Accuracy	Accuscript Accuracy
Horizontal Overlap Small	24.3%	2.9%
Horizontal Overlap Large	12.9%	2.4%
Vertical Overlap	27.8%	12.6%
Occlusion by wave	15.4%	10.5%
Occlusion by circles	35.9%	32.3%
Black Waves	16.3%	1.5%

For methods that consider hiding parts of images we considered several ways of placing the occlusions (middle of image, or determine the part of the image, middle, top or bottom, with the majority of black pixels and apply the occlusions where we have larger concentration of black pixels, or less black pixels), and also varying the size of occlusions (wave amplitude, wavelength, circle radius, or number of circles per image). In our current tests we were more focused on the overall results for each kind of transformation, and getting a feeling of which one works or not based on Gestalt assumptions and humans results, rather than varying the parameters for a particular one. Although we did some preliminary tests varying some parameters, we did not record a comparison among them. However, we picked the most convenient constraints discovered through experiments so far.

We observe that comparing against our previous results, some of the current methods performs better for some recognizers (i.e. for horizontal overlaps, and adding noise the form of black waves or lines). We shall explain here that the other transformations previously considered (Table 2) [16,17], were adding lines, grids, arcs, background noise, convolution masks and special filters, using variable stroke width, slope, rotations, stretching, compressing, and using lexicon challenges such as size, density, and availability. If we consider that with the previous approach we used up to three image transformations for each test image, then the new results may be considered better since we are using only one transformation. Most probably, combining more than one transformation will decrease the recognizers' accuracy even more.

Table 2. The accuracy of handwriting recognizers with previous image transformations

Word Recognizers	Accuracy
WMR	9.2%
Accuscript	4.4%

Another point we need to clarify is that due to the randomness of some parameters of our transformations, we may end up with images with just small areas affected by occlusions and mostly covering parts of the background. We should explain that most of the images correctly recognized by our handwriting recognizers are falling in this category. Fig. 9 shows several images that were correctly recognized but where the transformation chosen did not modify the original image too much and therefore did not add enough challenge to the recognition task. But on the other hand we have seen that for fairly clean images with well chosen parameters for transformations the recognizers would have difficulties (Fig. 3 through Fig. 7). In our future tests we will consider this aspect of the problem and try to eliminate those cases through a better selection of our parameters and transformations.

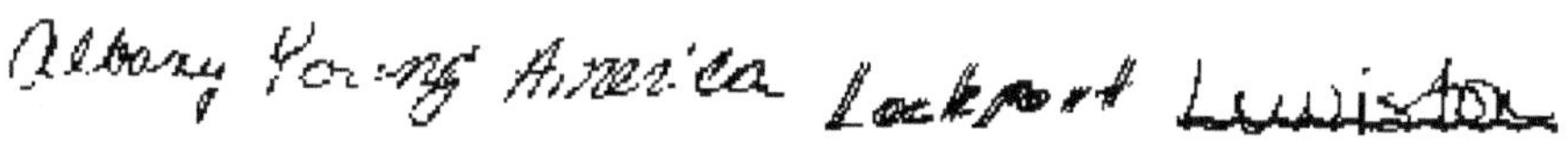

Fig. 9. Examples of handwritten images that were recognized by one of our testing recognizers. The truth words are: *Albany, Young America, Lockport, Lewiston*

We administered random sets of about 60 images each to be recognized by a number of 9 voluntary students from our department. The test consists of about 10 handwritten images per each one of the 6 transformations previously described. The images were chosen at random from the sets of about 4,100 deformed images per transformation. The human subjects were relatively familiar with the words in the images since they are city names from the US Western region. Our tests suggest that human performance depends on contextual known or linguistic context, and prior knowledge of the word provides the greatest advantage to human readers, therefore memory and word familiarity as Gestalt principles have proven to be valid clues for humans. Usually, if the original handwritten sample was clean to begin with, after deformation it did not create problems for humans to recognize the word, but machines failed. However, if the original sample contained noise or was poor written or captured, then even the original one caused problem to both human and computer, not to mention after deformation. Therefore most of the human errors came from junk original images rather than difficulties with the deformations applied on those images. The human results are presented in Table 3 and we could conclude that vertical overlaps and occlusions by white or black waves or lines are the least problematic for humans. For occlusion by circles we could explain the lower accuracy by imagining that some occlusions perhaps covered large part of a letter or the entire letter, as well as for larger space between the words that overlap on horizontal causing to misleading words as shown in a previous example (Fig. 8).

Table 3. The accuracy of human readers

Human Tests	All Deforms	Horizontal Overlap (Small)	Horizontal Overlap (Large)	Vertical Overlap	Occlusion by waves	Occlusion by circles	Black Waves
Images	534	90	89	88	87	90	90
Accuracy	76.2%	76.6%	65.1%	87.5%	80.4%	67.7%	80.0%

Both humans' and handwriting recognizers' accuracy were computed as the percentages of entirely recognized images. The CAPTCHA tests are fully graded pass or fail, where pass is granted when all the characters of the word were correctly recognized, and fail otherwise.

In general, the recognition of unconstrained handwriting is difficult because of the great variability in writing styles, spacing between words and lines, character sizes, and shape similarity. Different types of printing and background clarity also add to this challenge [18]. Moreover, the accuracy of handwriting recognizers is dependent upon the size and density of the lexicon, and mainly its availability [21,23]. For our tests purpose and to give machines a fair shot, we consider here a lexicon of size equal to the number of test images, containing all the truth words, and we did not consider increasing the lexicon density. However, for a general unconstrained example we should consider a large subset of English dictionary or the entire one, or move to the lexicon free approaches. In these cases, clearly the recognizers accuracy would drastically further decrease.

5   Summary and Future Work

Evaluating our handwritten image challenges would reveal that they satisfy all the requirements to be a CAPTCHA: *i)* there is no risk of image repetition since the image generation is completely automated, the words, images and distortions chosen at random; *ii)* the transformed images cannot be easily normalized or rendered noise free by present computer programs (i.e. handwriting recognizers, OCRs), although original handwritten images must be public knowledge; *iii)* the deformed images do not pose problems to humans, whereas the handwritten CAPTCHA images remain unbroken by the state-of-the-art recognizers throughout our tests. Therefore, our handwritten CAPTCHA could be successfully used as a biometric for online services to prove humanity and aliveness, and to defend online services against malicious attacks.

We have described several new ways of creating Handwritten CAPTCHA. Starting with the Gestalt psychology, we analyzed the image transformations that use gestalt components and tested various sets of images on two handwriting recognizers. The results obtained so far have been encouraging, thus the perspectives of even better results in the future are possible. We will reconsider some of the transformations and vary the parameters or use a combination of them in order to lower the recognizer accuracy. This kind of tests does not contradict with the rules of automatic tests generated by computers since we always ensure some level of randomness to be preserved. Some more work is needed for tests on human subjects to determine how much is loosing in the recognition rate for complicated (highly distorted) handwritten samples. Collecting clean handwritten samples of high frequency words in English will be a priority in our future research, since common used words are tided to visual memory and could provide good hints for humans and be straightforward to read in most deformed circumstances, but remain clueless for machines that do not make any difference among words in English dictionary. Alternatively, we will consider constructing handwritten word images by gluing together characters randomly chosen from our sets of handwritten character images of isolated upper and lower case alphabet. In addition, a handwriting distorter for generating manifold samples from a handwritten word could be used to generate million of fresh different testing images.

References

1. Altavista add url site. altavista.com/sites/addurl/newurl
2. L. von Ahn, M. Blum, and J. Langford.: Telling humans and computers apart (automatically) or how lazy cryptographers do *AI*. Technical Report TR CMU-CS-02-117. (2002)

3. H. Baird and K. Popat: Human interactive proofs and document image analysis. Proc. IAPR 2002 Workshop on Document Analysis Systems. (2002)
4. M. Blum, L. von Ahn, J. Langford, and N. Hopper: The captcha project: Completely automatic public turing test to tell computers and humans apart. http://www.captcha.net. (2000)
5. Captcha project. http://www.captcha.net.
6. M. Chew and H. Baird. Baffletext: A human interactive proof. Proc. SPIE-IST Electronic Imaging, Document Recognition and Retrieval. (2003) 305–316
7. A. Coates, H. Baird, and R. Fateman: Pessimal print: a reverse turing test. Proc. IAPR 6th International Conference on Document Analysis and Recognition. (2001) 1154–1158
8. J. T. Favata: Character model word recognition. Proc. Fifth InternationalWorkshop on Frontiers in Handwriting Recognition. (1996) 437–440
9. G. Kim and V. Govindaraju: A lexicon driven approach to handwritten word recognition for real-time applications. IEEE Transactions on Pattern Analysis and Machine Intelligence. 19(4) (1997) 366–379
10. G. Kochanski, D. Lopresti, and C. Shih: A reverse turing test using speech. Proc. International Conference on Spoken Language Processing. (2002)
11. K. Koffka: Principles of Gestalt Psychology. Harcourt Brace. (1935)
12. S. Madhvanath and V. Govindaraju: The role of holistic paradigms in handwritten word recognition. IEEE Transactions on Pattern Analysis and Machine Intelligence. 23(2) (2001)
13. G. Mori and J. Malik: Breaking a visual captcha. Computer Vision and Pattern Recognition. (2003)
14. S. Rice, G. Nagy, and T. Nartker: Optical character recognition: An illustrated guide to the frontier. (1999)
15. Y. Rui and Z. Liu: Artifacial: Automated reverse turing test using facial features. Proc. The 11th ACM International Conference on Multimedia. (2003)
16. A. Rusu, and V. Govindaraju: Handwritten CAPTCHA: Using the difference in the abilities of humans and machines to read handwritten words. Ninth IAPR International Workshop on Frontiers of Handwriting Recognition. (2004)
17. A. Rusu, and V. Govindaraju: Handwriting Word Recognition: A New CAPTCHA Challenge. Fifth International Conference on Knowledge Based Computer Systems. (2004)
18. A. Senior and A. Robinson: An off-line cursive handwriting recognition system. IEEE Transactions on Pattern Analysis and Machine Intelligence. 20(3) (1998) 309–321
19. A. Turing: Computing machinery and intelligence. Mind. 59(236) (1950) 433–460
20. J. Xu, R. Lipton, I. Essa, M. Sung, and Y. Zhu: Mandatory human participation: A new authentication scheme for building secure systems. ICCCN. (2003)
21. H. Xue and V. Govindaraju: On the dependence of handwritten word recognizers on lexicons. IEEE Transactions on Pattern Analysis and Machine Intelligence. 24(12) (2002) 1553–1564
22. H. Xue and V. Govindaraju: A stochastic model combining discrete symbols and continuous attributes and its applications to handwriting recognition. International Workshop on Document Analysis and Systems. (2002) 70–81
23. H. Xue, V. Govindaraju, and P. Slavik: Use of lexicon density in evaluating word recognizers. IEEE Transactions on Pattern Analysis and Machine Intelligence. 24(6) (2002) 789–800

Characters or Faces: A User Study on Ease of Use for HIPs

Yong Rui, Zicheng Liu, Shannon Kallin, Gavin [anke, and Cem Paya

{yongrui, zliu, shannonk, gavinj, cemp}@microsoft.com

Abstract. Web-based services designed for human users are being abused by computer programs (bots). This real-world issue has recently generated a new research area called Human Interactive Proofs (HIP), whose goal is to defend services from malicious attacks by differentiating bots from human users. During the past few years, while more than a dozen HIP systems have been developed, there is little user study been done in evaluating HIP's ease of use and friendliness. In this paper, we first introduce a new HIP based on human face detection, and then report a comparative user study between this new face HIP and a more conventional character-based HIP. Study results show that the users are almost equally divided in evaluating their overall ease of use.

1 Introduction

Web services are increasingly becoming part of people's everyday life. For example, we use free email accounts to send and receive emails; we use online polls to gather people's opinion; and we use chat rooms to socialize with others. But all these Web services designed for human use are being abused by automated computer programs (bots). Malicious programmers have designed bots to register thousands of free email accounts every minute [1,3]. Bots have been used to cast votes in online polls [1]. Chat rooms and online shopping are being abused by bots as well [2, 7].

These real-world issues have recently generated a brand-new research area called Human Interactive Proofs (HIP), whose goal is to defend services from malicious attacks by differentiating bots from human users. The first idea related to HIP can be traced back to Naor who wrote an unpublished note in 1996 [7]. The first HIP system in action was developed in 1997 by researchers at Alta Vista [2]. Its goal was to prevent bots from adding URLs to the search engine to skew the search results. In recent years, more than a dozen HIP algorithms and systems have been developed, most of which are based on characters [1,3]. These character-based HIPs are main streams in today's commercial deployment, e.g., Yahoo, MSN Passport, etc. They mainly explore the gap between human and bots in terms of reading poorly printed or manipulated characters. Figure 1 shows a character HIP used in MSN Passport, which consists of distorted characters and random arcs. A user needs to recognize the characters and correctly types in the space below the HIP to prove he/she is a human.

H.S. Baird and D.P. Lopresti (Eds.): HIP 2005, LNCS 3517, pp. 53-65, 2005.
© Springer-Verlag Berlin Heidelberg 2005

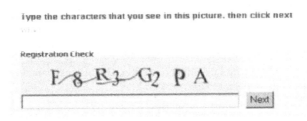

Fig. 1. An example character HIP

The MSN Passport HIP is similar to other character HIP in that it uses distorted and manipulated texts. However, it has an additional defense due to its segmentation difficulty, e.g., the arcs [4]. We will use this particular character HIP to represent the class of character HIPs in the rest of this paper.

Character HIPs are the mostly widely used HIPs in today's commercial sites, because of their ease of use, ease of implementation and universality. The "universality" property requires a HIP to be usable by people from different countries. An English-digit based audio HIP, for example, does not satisfy the universality property as people who do not understand English cannot use the HIP. Universality is especially important in practice as it eliminates the localization effort for sites such as Yahoo or MSN. (See [8] for other good HIP properties).

We recently developed a HIP, which is completely different from character HIPs, yet also satisfies the universality property. This new HIP is based on human face and facial feature detection. In fact, it is even more universal than character HIPs, as people all know human faces, regardless where they come from. On the other hand, face detection and facial feature (e.g., eyes, mouth, nose, etc.) detection have been very difficult for machines, even after decades of research. Non-frontal faces, asymmetrical faces, dim/bright lighting conditions, and cluttered background make the task even more difficult for machines, while human have no problem in those situations. In [8], we reported detailed experiments on the robustness of the face HIP to malicious attacks from the best face detectors [5,11,12] and facial feature detectors [9] available today. Results show that the face HIP is robust at a rate of 2 out of a million. For details of the algorithms and attacks, the readers are referred to [8]. In this paper will concentrate on the use-friendliness aspect of the face HIP.

The face HIP works as follows. Per each user request, it automatically synthesizes an image with a distorted face embedded in a clustered background. The user is asked to first find the face and then click on 4 points (2 eyes and 2 mouth corners) on the face. If the user can correctly identify these points, the face HIP concludes the user is a human; otherwise, the user is a machine.

During the past few years, while more than a dozen HIP systems have been developed, there is little user study been done in evaluating HIP's ease of use and friendliness. But in reality, ease of use is as important as the robustness (to attack) of a HIP. Good user experience is becoming increasingly important as HIPs are not only used in one-time activities (e.g., registering an account), but also in *recurring* transactions (e.g., challenge-response systems against spam). In this paper, we will report a comparative user study between this face HIP and the MSN character HIP. Study results show that the users are almost equally divided between the two HIPs in terms of overall experience. The rest of the paper is organized as follows. In Section 2, we describe the face HIP. In Section 3, we discuss the user study design and methodology. We present the study results in Section 4 and give concluding remarks in Section 5.

2   The Face HIP

The details on how to create the face HIP is reported in [8]. For completeness of this paper, we give a brief description of the HIP algorithm in this section.

Human faces are arguably the most familiar object to humans, rendering it possibly the best candidate for HIP. Regardless of nationalities, culture differences or educational background, we all recognize human faces. In fact, our ability is so good that we can recognize human faces even if they are distorted, partially occluded, or in bad lighting conditions.

Computer vision researchers have long been interested in developing automated face detection algorithms. A good survey paper on this topic is [10]. In general face detection algorithms can be classified into four categories: knowledge-based, feature-based, template matching, appearance-based. So far, the fourth approach is the most successful one [10].

In spite of decades of hard research on face and facial feature detection, today's best detectors still suffer from several main limitations including the assumption that **faces are symmetric**, the difficulties of handling arbitrary **head rotations**, **arbitrary lighting**, and **cluttered background**. These conditions are among the most difficult cases for automated face detection, yet we human seldom have any problem under those conditions. If we use the above 4 conditions to design a HIP test, it can take advantage of the large detection gap between human and machine. Indeed, this gap motivates our design of the face HIP.

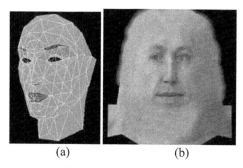

(a)   (b)

Fig. 2. (a) The 3D wire model of a generic head. (b) The cylindrical head texture map of an arbitrary person

We next use a concrete example to illustrate how to automatically generate a face HIP test image, taking into account of the 4 conditions discussed above. For clarity, we use F to indicate a foreground object in an image, e.g., a face; B to indicate the background in an image; I to indicate the whole image (i.e., foreground and background); and T to indicate cylindrical texture map.

[**Procedure**] Generating a face HIP test image

[**Input**] The only inputs to our algorithm are the 3D wire model of a generic head (see Figure 2 (a)) and a 512 x 512 cylindrical texture map Tm of an arbitrary person (see Figure 2 (b)). Note that any person's texture map will work in our system and from that single texture map we can in theory generate infinite number of test images.

[**Output**] A 320 x 320 test image I_F (see Figure 5) with ground truth (i.e., face location and facial feature locations).

1. Confusion texture map Tc generation

    This process takes advantage of the **Cluttered Background** limitation to design the HIP test. The 512 x 512 confusion texture map Tc (see Figure 3) is obtained by moving facial features (e.g., eyes, nose and mouth) in Figure 2 (b) to different places such that the "face" no longer looks like a face.

2. Global head transformation

    Because we have the 3D wire model (see Figure 2 (a)), we can easily generate any global head transformations we want. Specifically, the transformations include translation, scaling, and rotation of the head. Translation controls where we want to position the head in the final image I_F. Scaling controls the size of the head, and rotation can be around all the three x, y, and z axes. At run time, we randomly select the global head transformation parameters and apply them to the 3D wire model texture-mapped with the input texture Tm. This process takes advantage of the **Head Orientations** limitation to design the HIP test.

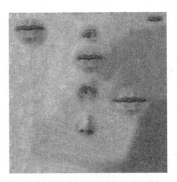

Fig. 3. The confusion texture map Tc, is generated by randomly moving facial features (e.g., eyes, nose and mouth) in Fig 2 (b) to different places such that the "face" no longer looks like a face

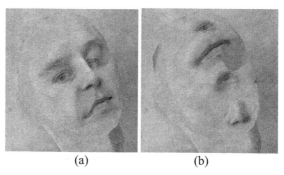

(a)   (b)

Fig. 4. (a) The head after global transformation and facial feature deformation. We denote this head by F_h. (b) The confusion head after global transformation and facial feature deformation. We denote this head by Fc

3. Local facial feature deformations

The local facial feature deformations are used to modify the facial feature positions so that they are slightly deviated from their original positions and shapes. This deformation process takes advantage of the **Face Symmetry** limitation to design the HIP test. Each geometric deformation is represented as a vector of vertex differences. We have designed a set of geometric deformations including the vertical and horizontal translations of the left eye, right eye, left eyebrow, right eyebrow, left mouth corner, and right mouth corner. Each geometric deformation is associated with a random coefficient uniformly distribution in [-1, 1], which controls the amount of deformation to be applied. At run time, we randomly select the geometric deformation coefficients and apply them to the 3D wire model. An example of a head after Steps 2 and 3 is shown in Figure 4 (a). Note that the head has been rotated and facial features deformed.

4. Confusion texture map transformation and deformation

In this step, we conduct exactly the same Steps 2 and 3 to the confusion texture map Tc, instead to Tm. This step generates the transformed and deformed confusion head Fc as shown in Figure 4 (b).

5. Stage-1 image I_1 generation

Use the confusion texture map Tc as the background B and use F_h as the foreground to generate the 320 x 320 stage-1 image I_1 [8].

6. Stage-2 image I_2 generation

Make L copies of randomly shrunk Tc and randomly put them into image I_1 to generate the 320 x 320 stage-2 image I_2 [8]. This process takes advantage of the **Cluttered Background** limitation to design the HIP test. Note that none of the copies should occlude the key face regions including eyes, nose and mouth.

7. Final test image I_F generation (Figure 5)

There are three steps in this stage. First, make M copies of the confusion head Fc and randomly put them into image I_2. This step takes advantage of the Cluttered

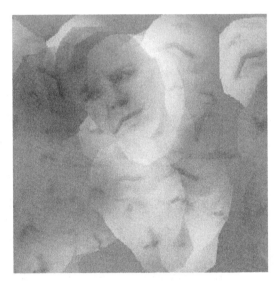

Fig. 5. An example face HIP test image

Background limitation. Note that none of the copies should occlude the key face regions including eyes, nose and mouth. Second, we now have $M+1$ regions in the image, where M of them come from Fc and one from F_h. Let $Avg(m)$, $m = 0$, ..., $M+1$, be the average intensity of region m. We next re-map the intensities of each region m such that $Avg(m)$'s are uniformly distributed in [0,255] across the $M+1$ regions, i.e., some of the regions become darker and others become brighter. This step takes advantage of the Lighting and Shading limitation.

The above 7 steps take the 4 face detection limitations into account and generate the face HIP test images that are very difficult for face detectors. In [8], we reported detailed experiments on the robustness of the face HIP to malicious attacks from the best face detectors [5,11,12] and facial feature detectors [9] available today. Results show that the face HIP is robust at a rate of 2 out of a million. In the following section, we will report another aspect of the HIP – its ease of use and friendliness.

3 User Study Design and Methodology

We recruited 200 panelists from an independent research panel. To eliminate gender difference, the panelists are 50% male and 50% female. They also have different levels of internet experience, ranging from beginner, to intermediate, to advanced. Furthermore, the panelists have diverse income levels to eliminate another potential bias factor. The panelists voluntarily participate in the user study online from their own homes. This not only ensures that they do not need to change their regular online behavior, but also ensures that they are viewing the HIP images in the settings they would be most comfortable with, e.g., monitor type and size, screen resolution, contrast and brightness, etc.

The section of user study on comparing HIPs is part of a larger-scale study that concerns with other issues in MSN Passport registration (see the study flow chart in Figure 6). In the study before the HIP section, the panelists go through a regular MSN Passport registration process. As a result, the section on comparing HIPs is in full context and the panelists already know how to register in Passport and understand the purpose of putting a HIP test inside the registration process.

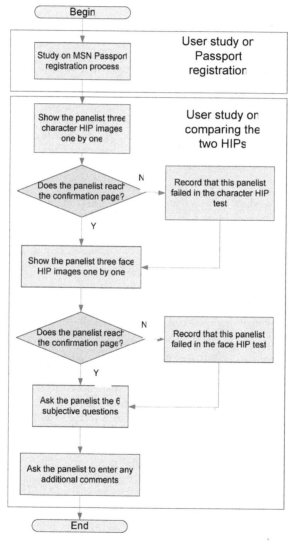

Fig. 6. The flow chart of the user study. The first part of the study is on Passport registration generic issues, which is outside the scope of this paper. The second part of the study is on comparing the two HIPs. The first study does set up the context for the second study

In the study, we use two measures to evaluate each HIP's performance, i.e., objective task performance, and subjective responses. The latter includes asking various questions to the panelists. The list of questions and panelists' responses are reported in detail in Section 4. The scenario of the objective task is at an MSN Passport registration page. The panelists are given the following instructions:

*Qou may recall that at one point during the registration processes you've &ist evaluated, you were re⬚uired to input some letters and numbers that were **"distorted."***

*This is a **safety feature**, the purpose of which is to prevent automated computer programs from generating thousands of fake e-mail accounts in order to send unsolicited IspamI mail. (omputers have a difficult time identifying distorted letters within an image.*

In the last 2 tasks we'd like you to take a closer look at this IcharacterI distortion and compare it with an alternative IfacesI distortion that has been developed. As you review both versions, please imagine that you are in the middle of a registration process, similar to those which you have &ist evaluated. Qou do not need to fill out the registration form, simply evaluate the images.

Specifically, the panelists are asked to conduct the following task:

Without completing the registration form, please scroll down the page until you can see the image, then follow the instructions to interact with the image appropriately. Make sure that you click the Ine⬚I button to cycle through the multiple images you will be shown.

Figure 6. The flow chart of the user study. The first part of the study is on Passport registration generic issues, which is outside the scope of this paper. The second part of the study is on comparing the two HIPs. The first study does set up the context for the second study.

If a panelist can successful pass the HIP test, by clicking on the "next" button, he/she will be presented with a similar page, but with a different HIP image. This process iterates for three (3) images. Once the panelist correctly finishes the 3rd HIP image, he/she will be greeted with a "Congratulation/Confirmation" page, indicating that he/she has finished the task. The group of 3 images can both be the character HIP and the face HIP. This "objective task" gives us an *ob&ctive* way to see if a particular HIP is easy to use – the higher the percentage of the panelists who can reach the Confirmation page, the easier the HIP is.

4   User Study Results

After finishing the *ob&ctive* task, the panelist will then be given six (6) *sub&ctive* questions. For each question, the panelist selects a number from 1 to 7, 1 being the most "disagree" with the question, and 7 being the most "agree" with the question. For the ease of presenting results in the paper, we classify scales 1 and 2 being "Oppose", scales 3-5 being "Neutral", and scales 6-7 being "Support". In addition to the above 1-7 scale answers, we also provide panelists with a field where they can enter free-form comments (see Figure 6).

We next report the exact questions asked and the detailed results. There are two types of questions. Overall-quality questions (Q1, Q2, Q5 and Q6) evaluate the overall performance, e.g., ease of use, of a HIP. On the other hand, specific questions (Q3 and Q4) are designed to reveal more detailed findings.

4.1 Overall Findings

We classify the overall findings into two categories: "Ease of Use" and "If should Use". The results on "Ease of Use" are summarized in Table 1. The following observations can be made.

In the HIP comparison, users are split in terms of overall preference for the characters HIP and the face HIP. The levels of Ease of Use are similar for the two HIPs, not only verified by the objective task but also the subjective responses.

In fact, both Ease of Understanding Instructions ($\square$1: How difficult or easy was it to understand the instructions for interacting with the images?) and Ease of Performing Task ($\square$2: How difficult or easy was it to perform this task on the "faces" version?) are similar for the two HIPs.

Table 1.   Overall findings: Ease of Use   (* % based on responses of 6-7 on 7-point scales)

Metric	Character	Face
Objective task Success on task (reached confirmation page)	80%	78%
Ease of Understanding Instructions ? $\square$1: How difficult or easy was it to understand the instructions for interacting with the images? (1 = Extremely difficult and 7 = Extremely easy)	87%	82%
Ease of Performing Task ? $\square$2: How difficult or easy was it to perform this task on the "faces" version? (1 = Extremely difficult and 7 = Extremely easy)	78%	77%

Table 2. Which HIP we should use

Metric	Support	Neutral	Oppose
Character	56%	38%	7%
Face	47%	34%	19%

There are two questions on "If should use". For question □5: Between the character HIP and the face HIP of the security feature you just reviewed, which one did you like better?, 53% prefer the face HIP and 47% prefer the character HIP – again, no significant difference between the two HIPs.

For question □6: In your opinion, should Microsoft .NET Passport use the "characters"/"faces" version for users registering a Hotmail account? (1 = I would strongly oppose this and 7 = I would strongly support this), the results are listed in Table 2.

As shown in Table 2, there are 7% users who oppose character HIP. We speculate that these users either think the characters are too difficult to recognize or they don't think HIP is necessary in general. Additional research needs to be done to understand why 7% of users oppose character HIP.

It is interesting to note that there are significantly more people who oppose face HIP. From the interviews with the users, we find that some of the users who oppose face HIP think the distorted faces are offensive to them. There are another set of users who do not mind the images themselves, but they feel that the images might be offensive to other people. How to design a face HIP so that it is visually less disturbing yet difficult for bots is an interesting problem.

To summarize, although the panelists are almost equally divided on "Ease of use", they have mixed comments on "If should use" -- while more panelists (53% vs. 47%) like the face HIP, more panelists (19% vs. 7%) oppose the idea of using it. This interesting bi-modal distribution shows up again in "specific findings" in Section 4.2.1. We speculate that panelists like the face HIP because of the "seek and find then click" aspect of the task -- most panelists prefer *clicking* to *typing*. Therefore, perhaps it is the nature of the task that is liked and not the specific stimulus.

4.2 Specific Findings

4.2.1 Pleasant or Not

This question is designed to reveal if distortion (of characters/faces) will pose trouble on the panelists. □3: How would you rate the images of the "faces"? (1 = Very disturbing and 7 = Very pleasant)

Table 3. Pleasant or not

	Pleasant (6-7)	Neutral (3-5)	Disturbing (1-2)
Character	40%	48%	2%
Face	39%	44%	17%

17% panelist rated the face HIP as disturbing (1-2) while only 2% said the same for the character HIP. It is interesting that the panelists have a bi-modal distribution: while some commented that the faces were strange or eerie, other thought it was fun and interesting:

Eerie:
- *"It is a bit eerie to look at."*
- *"It's a little freaky looking...kinda spooky."*
- *"Don't like it, disturbing."*
- *"The faces are very creepy. The images look like severed heads."*

Fun:
- *"It seems very effective and fun for kids."*
- *"It seems a really secure and it's fun to do also."*
- *"It was interesting, and kind of cool."*
- *"I found it entertaining and useful at the same time."*

4.2.2 Size and Area

We speculate that some panelists may think the areas of the HIP images maybe too big or too small. ☐4: How would you rate the area you had to click on the image? (1 = Far too small and 7 = Far too large). The majority of panelists did not have an issue with the size / area of the characters or faces (see Table 4).

Table 4. Is the image size too large or too small

	Too large	Neutral	Too small
Character	21%	79%	1%
Face	14%	84%	3%

4.2.3 Difficulties with Both HIPs

For the character HIP, majority found it easy to read; however, certain letters gave them trouble when lines ran across the image (see circled area in Figure 7)

Fig. 7. An example where the character HIP can be difficult for human

- *"The characters were easy to read, and the whole process was easy to complete."*
- *"The H looks an awful lot like the N...especially when there is a line of some sort running through."*
- *"The F's and E's can be difficult to see with the lines through them."*

For the face HIP, most users did not find it difficult to accomplish; also, some panelists mentioned that they preferred clicking on the image to typing in the characters

- *"That was surprisingly much faster and easier."*
- *"It was fast and easy. I could see the face clear."*
- *"Quicker than having to type the characters. Seems to be very easy."*
- *"This was much simpler than typing of characters."*

5 Conclusions and Discussions

In this paper, we reported a comparative user study between a character HIP and a new face HIP, and have the following major findings:

- For the objective task, the panelists performed almost equally well for the two HIPs.
- For "Ease of use", the panelists rated both HIPs similarly on both the ease of performing the task and understanding the instruction of the task.
- For "If should use", while more panelists (53% vs. 47%) liked the face HIPs, there were also more panelists (19% vs. 7%) opposes the idea of using it in Passport registration page.
- There was a bi-modal distribution in panelists when asking them if the face HIP images were pleasant. While some thought the images were eerie, other thought they were fun.
- Panelists thought the size/area of both HIP images were appropriate.
- Some panelists thought the character HIPs were difficult to solve, and others prefer the face HIP (clicking) to character HIP (typing).

As the state of art on OCR technology rapidly advances, it is becoming increasingly difficult to design a character-based HIP that can be difficult for computers yet easy for humans. For example, the Gimpy HIP used at Yahoo site was broken by Mori and Malik [6], and an earlier version of MSN Passport HIP was also broken [4]. Given that face detection from images has been a difficult task for computer vision researchers for many decades, face detection and facial feature detection may be a better candidate for robust HIPs.

While the new face HIP posses many attractive features, e.g., ease of use, universality, etc., some users thought it is eerie. It will be an interesting research direction to design a HIP that has all the nice features of the current face HIP, yet is less disturbing to sensitive users.

6 Acknowledgement

We would like to thank Vividence Research for helping conduct the user study.

References

1. Ahn, L., Blum, M., and Hopper, N. [., Telling humans and computers apart (Automatically) or How lazy cryptographers do AI, Technical Report CMU-CS-02-117, February, 2002
2. AltaVista's Add URL site: altavista.com/sites/addurl/newurl
3. Baird, H.S., and Popat, K., Human Interactive Proofs and Document Image Analysis," Proc., 5th IAPR Workshop on Document Analysis Systems, Princeton, N[, August 19-21, 2002
4. Chellapilla K., and Simard P., Using Machine Learning to Break Visual Human Interaction Proofs (HIPs), *Advances in Neural Information wrocessing Systems 1R*, Neural Information Processing Systems (NIPS'2004), MIT Press.
5. Colmenarez A. and Huang, T. S., Face detection with information-based maximum discrimination, Proc. of IEEE CVPR, pp., 782-788, 1997
6. Mori, G. and Malik , [., Recognizing objects in adversarial clutter: breaking a visual CAPTHA, CVPR 2003, pp. I 134-141.
7. Naor, M., Verification of a human in the loop or identification via the Turing test, unpublished notes, September 13, 1996
8. Rui, Y. and Liu, Z., ARTiFACIAL: Automated Reverse Turing test using FACIAL features, ACM/Springer Multimedia Systems [ournal, May 2004
9. Yan, S. C., Li, M. [., Zhang, H. [., and Cheng., Q. S., Ranking Prior Likelihoods for Bayesian Shape Localization Framework, Submitted to IEEE ICCV 2003.
10. Yang, M., Kriegman, D., and Ahuja, N., Detecting faces in images: a survey, IEEE Trans. on Pattern analysis and machine intelligence, Vol. 24, No. 1, [anuary 2002.
11. Yang, M., Roth, D., and Ahuja, N., A SNoW-Based Face Detector, Advances in Neural Information Processing Systems 12 (NIPS 12), S.A. Solla, T.K. Leen and K.-R. Muller (eds), pp. 855--861, MIT Press, 2000.
12. Zhang, Z., Zhu, L., Li, S. and Zhang, H, Real-time multiview face detection, Proc. Int'l Conf. Automatic Face and Gesture Recognition, pp. 149-154, 2002

Collaborative Filtering CAPTCHAs

Monica Chew and J.D. Tygar*

University of California, Berkeley
{mmc,tygar}@cs.berkeley.edu

A bstract. Current CAPTCHAs require users to solve objective questions such as text recognition or image recognition. We propose a class of CAPTCHAs based on collaborative filtering. Collaborative filtering CAPTCHAs allow us to ask questions that have no absolute answer; instead, the CAPTCHAs are graded by comparison to other people's answers. We analyze the security requirements of collaborative filtering CAPTCHAs and find that although they are not ready to use now, collaborative filtering CAPTCHAs are worthy of further investigation.

1 Introduction

This paper proposes a framework for CAPTCHAs using collaborative filtering. By observing real-world trends made by human subjects, collaborative filtering CAPTCHAs attempt to extract complex patterns that reflect human choices. For example, humans who like a particular joke, such as a subtle pun, may also enjoy other jokes that incorporate similar patterns of whimsy, word-play, and ironic observation. We consider the proposition that these patterns are sufficiently complex that no computer agent can predict these patterns with equal accuracy. While one might naively believe that detecting patterns of humor is beyond the capability of any machine, we show in this paper that computer agents can do better than one might at first think. We conduct an experiment that demonstrates that joke-affinity CAPTCHAs can be weakly effective. Our results show that collaborative filtering CAPTCHAs, while not ready to use now, show promise beyond traditional CAPTCHA approaches and deserve further examination.

Why should we study collaborative filtering CAPTCHAs? Because current CAPTCHA research resembles an arms race between CAPTCHA developers and CAPTCHA attackers. CAPTCHA developers propose schemes which they hope are unbreakable, and CAPTCHA attackers break them. The text-recognition CAPTCHA EZ-Gimpy exemplifies this cycle [2]. EZ-Gimpy requires humans to transcribe an image containing a single English word. In 2003, Mori and Malik broke EZ-Gimpy with 87% success [10]. The Mori-Malik attack requires a dictionary. EZ-Gimpy designers then proposed a variation on EZ-Gimpy called

---

* This work was supported in part by the US Postal Service and the National Science Foundation. The opinions here are those of the authors and do not necessarily reflect the opinions of the funding sponsors.

H.S. Baird and D.P. Lopresti (Eds.): HIP 2005, LNCS 3517, pp. 66–81, 2005.

Gimpy-R which uses random character strings instead of English text, thus defeating a dictionary attack. Moy et al. broke Gimpy-R in 2004 with 78% success, and EZ-Gimpy using the same technique with 99% success [11].

Using collaborative filtering can make CAPTCHAs more difficult to break. Suppose we can develop a CAPTCHA where the attacker must derive CAPTCHA answers from other humans instead of solving an objective machine vision question such as text recognition. In theory, the only way to break such a CAPTCHA would be for the attacker to perform a user study and analyze the results, a very expensive proposition.

This paper contains the following contributions:

- We propose a collaborative filtering framework for CAPTCHAs.
- We propose new attack models on collaborative filtering CAPTCHAs.
- We give security requirements for input data to collaborative filtering CAPTCHAs.
- We present the results of an experiment on collaborative filtering CAPTCHAs.
- We give a list of open problems for further examination.

Section 2 describes collaborative filtering and its challenges. Section 3 outlines how to use collaborative filtering to build a CAPTCHA. Section 4 explains using Singular Vector Decomposition to predict user ratings. Section 5 describes experiments using the Jester dataset. Section 6 analyzes attacks on collaborative filtering CAPTCHAs. Section 7 lists related work, and Section 8 concludes with open problems.

2   Collaborative Filtering

Collaborative filters, or recommender systems, use a database of user preferences to predict items or topics a new user might like or find useful [3, 14]. For example, Amazon allows users to rate items for sale on a scale from 1 to 10. A new user, Alice, is compared to existing users based on purchase or browsing history. Amazon compares the user preferences of neighbors, or users who are historically similar to Alice, to predict new items Alice might like and then recommends them.

Challenges in collaborative filtering include:

- Accuracy. The prediction of Alice's ratings must be accurate in order for the recommendations to be useful. Additionally, in a collaborative filtering CAPTCHA, inaccurate predictions will cause humans to fail the CAPTCHA.
- Sparsity. For very large recommender systems (e.g., Amazon, the Internet Movie Database, and Ebay), even a very prolific user might have preference data for a very small percentage of the items in the system. Sparsity makes predictions more difficult.
- Scalability. Because nearest-neighbor algorithms (to find users with similar preferences) scale in the number of users and items, very large recommender systems suffer scalability problems.

- "Polluted" data. Malicious or apathetic users may enter incorrect preference data, hampering the accuracy of prediction algorithms. Dellarocas has done some work in this area to reject "outliers" — however, this approach has the unwanted effect of unfairly rejecting users with eccentric tastes [5]. In general, the collaborative filtering research concentrates on improving the predictive accuracy in the absence of adversaries, so this challenge is not well-studied in comparison with the rest.

In this work, we are primarily concerned with accuracy and polluted data.

3   Collaborative Filtering CAPTCHAs

Previous CAPTCHAs require users to solve cognitive tasks such as text recognition and image recognition. Both of these tasks are currently subjects of machine vision research. Sophisticated machine vision attacks exist for text-based CAPTCHAs; it is only reasonable to expect the machine vision community to make progress in image recognition if these CAPTCHAs are adopted.

What if we could use challenge questions that have no absolute answer? Then we could build a CAPTCHA where the user is correct so long as enough known humans agree. Collaborative filtering allows us to do so. Collaborative filtering is a way to aggregate data from many different human users so that we can easily compare new data. The collaborative filtering approach differs from previous approaches in that the CAPTCHA designer does not know the correct answer initially, but measures the correct answer from human opinions. There are many subjective topics we could use to build a CAPTCHA: however, finding a good source of input data is an open problem for reasons we discuss below.

3.1   Sources of Data

To build a collaborative filtering CAPTCHA, we require a source of data that evokes some aspect of our humanity that is difficult to quantify. For example:

- Humans recognize quality in art (such as movies, music, literature, or images), and computers do not.
- Art (visual art, music) evokes human emotion which may be unpredictable by computers.
- Humans have philosophical leanings (political opinions, religious doctrines, etc.) which are difficult to codify.
- Humans recognize humor in jokes, and computers do not.

Choosing a good source of data is difficult. For example, building a CAPTCHA out of movie ratings presents two problems: movies are time-consuming and expensive for users to watch and rate, and online oracles such as the Internet Movie Database can be used by adversaries. Cultural bias can also plague collaborative filtering CAPTCHAs: the filter may only make accurate predictions for certain demographic groups. However, all existing CAPTCHAs (including those based on text and images) discriminate against a some demographic. Visually impaired or illiterate people cannot pass a reading-based CAPTCHA, for example.

3.2   Stages of the CAPTCHA

Given an appropriate topic that computers find difficult to evaluate, we can construct a CAPTCHA based on collaborative filtering. A collaborative filtering CAPTCHA goes through several phases:

- *Training.* In the training phase, a group of known humans rates documents in the gauge set. The seed data or training data will be used to generate predictions for new user who wish to take the CAPTCHA.
- *Testing.* The testing phase is entered whenever a new user wants to take a CAPTCHA. Suppose Alice wants to take the CAPTCHA. We present a strict subset of documents in the gauge set for Alice to rate. Based on Alice's ratings of the subset and the training data, we make predictions for Alice's ratings of the remainder of the gauge set. Alice then rates the remainder of the gauge set. We now have actual and predicted ratings for the remainder of the set. If the predicted ratings are close enough to the actual ratings, Alice passes. The threshold for passing is an open research problem.
- *Reseeding.* If Alice passes as human, the CAPTCHA enters the reseeding phase. Alice rates new documents that are not in the gauge set. If enough new users rate these documents, the new documents can be used as a new gauge set. Having dynamic data in the collaborative filter is important; recommendations and predictions of a small, static dataset are subject to attack.

Now we turn to the question of predicting ratings.

4   Using Singular Value Decomposition in Collaborative Filtering

Singular Value Decomposition (SVD) is a numerical method for doing collaborative filtering that separates user ratings by different features. A feature is an abstract notion that falls implicitly out of the decomposition; features require no special annotations in advance. Often, but not always, an abstract feature in the SVD corresponds to a real-world property of the item being rated. For example, one property of jokes is word-play. Users who find word-play humorous might prefer puns, and the word-play property might correspond to a particular feature in the decomposition. For the purposes of this experiment, the real properties corresponding to the features are irrelevant.

If the ratings matrix A holds ratings of users for documents, we can use SVD to decompose A: $A = USV^T$. A_{ij} is user i's rating of document j. It is useful to think of a row in U as a user's response vector, where U_{ik} is user i's response to feature k. S is the matrix of feature weights, or how important a feature is in determining the rating. S is 0 everywhere but the diagonal, where S_{kk} is the weight of feature k. V represents the amount of each feature in each document, so V_{jk} is the amount of feature k in document j. Since $S_{i \neq j} = 0$,

$$A_{ij} = \sum_k U_{ik} S_{kk} V_{jk}$$

Because of the way the SVD is computed, the first entry in S is the largest, so $S_{11} \gg S_{22} \gg \ldots \gg S_{nn}$. From this, we can estimate the ratings for a new user if we know that user's rating of the first document, R_1. From the previous equation, ignoring the new user's responses to other features, we have

$$R_1 = U_1 S_{11} V_{11}$$

We can then solve for U_1, the user's response to feature 1, and use that to estimate the ratings of other documents. As more ratings are known, the more feature responses we can estimate, and the more accurate the predictions become.

4.1   Measuring Error

The Mean Absolute Error is the error metric used most often in collaborative filtering literature. Let c be the number of jokes rated, p_{ij} be the prediction of user i's rating of joke j, and r_{ij} be the actual rating. Then MAE for user i is

$$MAE = \frac{1}{c} \sum_{j=1}^{c} |r_{ij} - p_{ij}|$$

It is useful to normalize this metric to the range of possible ratings, $[r_{max}, r_{min}]$ [7].

$$NMAE = \frac{MAE}{r_{max} - r_{min}}$$

4.2   Neighbors

Nearest-neighbor algorithms are commonly used to improve predictions using SVD. One way to measure how similar two user preferences are is to measure the distance between their preference vectors. Two users A and B are close if the cosine between their preference vectors is close to 1.

$$\cos\theta = \frac{A \cdot B}{\|A\|\|B\|}$$

One immediate problem with using nearest-neighbor algorithms in a CAPTCHA is that an adversary has fewer data points to guess in order to cheat successfully. We discuss security problems in more detail in Section 6.

5   Experiments with Collaborative Filtering CAPTCHAs

We have presented a class of CAPTCHAs based on collaborative filtering and shown how to implement them. In this section, we conduct two experiments and analyze the security requirements of collaborative filtering CAPTCHAs based on the results.

5.1   A Joke-Based Collaborative Filtering CAPTCHA

We chose to prototype a proof-of-concept collaborative filtering CAPTCHA based on jokes. The subject of jokes was chosen merely for convenience because a large dataset of joke ratings is publically available [6].

While the choice of jokes as the basis for our collaborative filter allowed us to prototype our system quickly, a collaborative filter based on jokes also suffers from a number of flaws. Jokes are often culturally biased, they are hard to generate by computer, and some jokes are offensive. As we discuss below, despite these drawbacks, the use of a joke-based collaborative filter did produce some interesting results and suggests that collaborative filtering deserves further research as an approach for building CAPTCHAs.

There are several possible approaches using jokes to build a CAPTCHA:

- Pick the best joke from a small set.
- Pick the worst joke from a small set.
- Rate the joke.

The third approach, rating the joke, is the most useful because it is the most general — the other two can be implemented based on the rating. If the user's assessment of the joke corresponds to the opinions of previous (human) users, the user passes the challenge. We can then optionally ask the user to rate new jokes and update the collaborative filter. Because this is a proof-of-concept CAPTCHA and because, to the best of our knowledge, this is the first collaborative filtering CAPTCHA, this experiment concentrated mainly on the accuracy of the collaborative filter.

The Jester project   The Jester project is a recommender system for jokes [6]. 24953 users in the system rated the same 10 jokes, or *gauge set*, on a scale from -10 (not funny) to 10 (funniest). Although up to 100 jokes were rated, we used only ratings from jokes in the gauge set in this experiment because the gauge set is dense.

To mitigate attacks on the collaborative filter, the data that users rate must fulfill two requirements:

- It must be large or renewable. The Jester system uses 100 jokes. It is possible to compose more jokes, however. If the data is too small, an adversary could simply use a human to rate all the jokes and "replay" known human answers.

– It must be uniformly distributed in quality. If the data does not follow a uniform distribution, an adversary could simply guess the most frequently-occurring rating.

Because neither of these requirements have an effect on the accuracy of predictions for legitimate users, we can disregard them for the purposes of predicting ratings.

5.2   Experiments with the Jester Dataset

In this experiment, we use ratings from the first eight jokes in the gauge set to predict ratings for the last two. We chose at random 100 users from 24953 to use as the training set. This training data was used to compute the feature weight and document matrices (S and V) in the SVD. Recall that S gives the weight of each feature, and V gives the amount of each feature in each document or joke. Because the training data is dense, small and fixed in this experiment, we avoided the problems of *sparsity* and *scalability* described in Section 2. Polluted data will always be a challenge in collaborative filtering CAPTCHAs — there is a trade-off between resistance to adversaries and unfairly failing users with unconventional preferences.

For the other 24853 users (the test data), we used the S and V matrices to predict the ratings of the last two jokes based on the ratings of the first 8. Additionally, all the ratings were normalized linearly to fall between 0 and 1.

Because initial accuracy of the CAPTCHA in distinguishing humans from machines does not depend on the third phase (*reseeding*) in a collaborative filtering CAPTCHA, reseeding is unimplemented.

Results The results of using all the training data without nearest neighbor algorithms to predict ratings for new users are shown in Figures 1 and 2. Figure 1 is a histogram of the cosine between the predicted ratings and the actual ratings for the last two jokes in the gauge set. Figure 2 shows the histogram of the NMAE for the predictions. The NMAE for a random prediction (distributed uniformly over the range) is 0.333 [7]. The NMAE using all the training data for predictions is 0.45, even higher than the expected NMAE for a random prediction.

Unfortunately, using the SVD decomposition of all 100 users in the training data was too inaccurate. Because there is much variation in joke preferences, the predictions were not good using all of the training data.

To improve predictions, we used only the ratings from the 10 nearest neighbors. For each user in the test set, we compared the user ratings for the first 8 jokes to all of the training data, using the cosine as the metric to find the 10 nearest neighbors. The SVD on the 10 nearest neighbors was used to predict the user's ratings for the remaining 2 jokes in the gauge set. Figures 4 and 3 show the results with nearest neighbor.

Figures 4 and 3 show that using nearest neighbors improves the predictions significantly. The NMAE with nearest-neighbor is 0.34, approximately the same

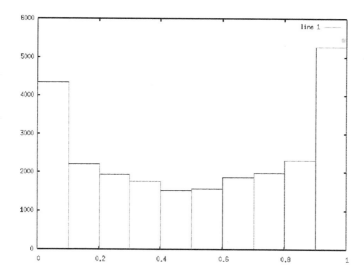

Fig. 1. A histogram of absolute values of cosines between predicted and actual ratings using SVD without nearest neighbor.

as the expected NMAE for random predictions. The NMAE is 0.187 using Eigentaste, the collaborative filtering algorithm developed by the designers of the Jester system [7]. The Eigentaste system uses Principal Component Analysis (PCA) in lieu of SVD. PCA allows dimensionality reduction for fast offline clustering of user preferences. Because this is a proof-of-concept CAPTCHA and the training data is small, PCA is unimplemented.

5.3   Visual Art and Emotions

In this section we describe a speculative collaborative filtering CAPTCHA that requires humans to specify emotions evoked by visual images. One measure for comparing emotions is the Russell circumplex model of affect, illustrated in Figure 5 [13]. The two principal axes are *excitement* and *pleasure*. Russell claimed these axes are orthogonal. For example, the emotion *distress* implies high excitement and displeasure, and so *distress* falls in the upper left quadrant of the model. However, low excitement and displeasure correspond to *depression* in the lower left quadrant. Emotions that are close to each other on the model are perceptually similar to humans, and vice versa. Opposite, or most dissimilar, emotions are diagonal to each other on the model [12].

To devise a CAPTCHA, we can require the user to rate the emotions of images as before and compare the predicted rating to the actual rating. However, SVD assumes a linear scale, not a circular one. As a first step, we can simply use the average rating (or emotion) to predict the rating of a new user, treating emotions as vectors on the unit circle.

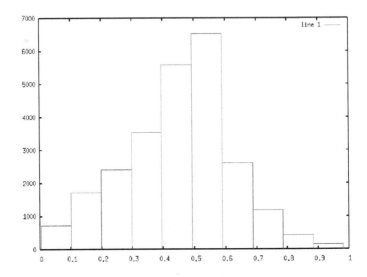

Fig. 2. A histogram of NMAE using SVD without nearest neighbor.

In a small experiment, we chose seven images from an online art gallery, and three random art images. A random art image is simply the result of coloring a random expression in two variables, where the color at a point (x, y) is determined by the value of the expression at that coordinate, as illustrated in Figure 6. Random art is a convenient source of input data to the collaborative filter because it is easy to generate.

Four test subjects chose emotions that best corresponded to the image. However, many of the images were not sufficiently evocative. All of the subjects had difficulty labelling the random art images. Additionally, the four test subjects differed widely on all but one image, where three out of four picked emotions in the same quadrant. Consequently, the average answers were not very meaningful. The result of this small experiment is that the data source that humans rate must be evocative. We also need numerical methods for collaborative filtering that work on higher-dimension scales.

6   Security Against Adversaries

Collaborative filtering CAPTCHAs are predicated on the unpredictability of human opinions. This condition could fail in several scenarios:

- The attacker (human or machine) infiltrates the training data. Then, to pass the CAPTCHA, the attacker can simply rate the gauge set as she did during the training phase. If training users complete the training phase remotely, we can require them to pass another type of CAPTCHA (e.g., an image recognition CAPTCHA) before entering the training phase.

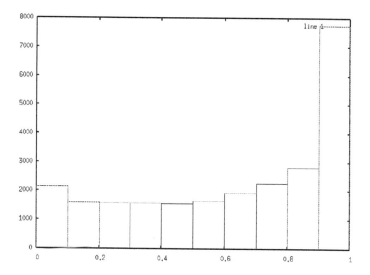

Fig. 3. A histogram of absolute values of cosines between predicted ratings and actual ratings from the SVD predictions with nearest neighbor.

- There is not enough variation in the jokes, i.e., the jokes are consistently no good (or conversely, the jokes are all very funny). In this case, the attacker simply rates each joke the average rating (which is predictable for a small number of jokes) to achieve a lower NMAE than random ratings. To defend against this attack, the ratings of the jokes in the gauge set must be uniformly distributed. The training phase can accomplish this by starting out with a large gauge set and eliminating jokes until the ratings are uniformly distributed. Similarly, in the reseeding phase, only new jokes that preserve the distribution are admitted to the gauge set.
- The attacker guesses a response vector that is consistent with the training data. The attacker then uses the reseeding phase to infiltrate the new gauge set. Of the attacks listed, this is the most insidious. The defense against this attack can include:

  - Introducing new jokes very frequently, so the gauge set is constantly changing.
  - Increasing the size of the gauge set.

From the experiments discussed in the previous section, there are several requirements on the data used for collaborative filtering:

- *Uniform.* Ratings for the data must be uniformly distributed. If the ratings show a bias (as in the case for the Jester dataset), an attacker can use that bias to pass more often than would be expected at random.

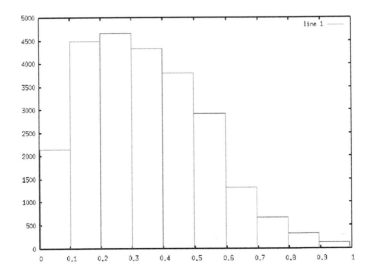

Fig. 4. A histogram of NMAE using nearest neighbor predictions.

- *Evocative.* The data must be sufficiently evocative. In the case of the CAPTCHA outlined in Section 5.3, the emotional effect of the images used was often unclear to the participants, diminishing the meaning of the ratings.
- *Dynamic.* The data must be renewable, or else the same data will appear to an attacker many times. In this case, a correct guess from the attacker will be very valuable, since the attacker can replay it many times.

Another important consideration is that collaborative filtering without using nearest neighbor algorithms failed. The purpose of predicting ratings with the entire training set instead of a subset was to amplify the difficulty of attack. Guessing or controlling the SVD of the entire training set is more difficult than doing the same for a small number of neighbors.

6.1   Exploiting Bias in Ratings

Let X be the user's ratings, Y be the predicted ratings, and $[r_{min}, r_{max}]$ be the range of ratings. In this section, we derive the NMAE between X and Y for three cases:

1. X and Y are uniform random variables. The NMAE for this case is presented in the Jester paper, but we generalize the derivation and show it to be independent of the range [7].
2. X and Y are normally distributed with mean μ and variances σ_x^2 and σ_y^2, respectively. The analysis of this case is summarized from the Jester paper.
3. X is normally distributed with mean μ and variance σ^2, $Y = \mu$. This comparison has not been presented previously.

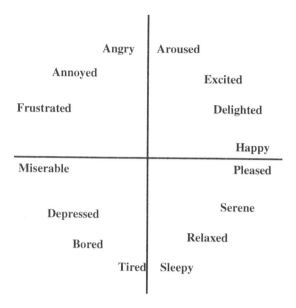

Fig. 5. Russell's circumplex model of emotion.

Uniform distribution Let X and Y be uniform random variables. The probability distribution of the error function $X - Y$ is triangular, ranging from $[r_{min}, r_{max}]$, where $f(x) = x + 20$ for $r_{min} \leq x \leq 0$, and $f(x) = 20 - x$ for $0 \leq x \leq r_{max}$. The probability distribution of the absolute error $|X - Y|$ gives the density function for the MAE. Taking the absolute value folds the function over the y-axis, giving the $f(x) = 20 - x$. Normalizing to integrate to 1, $f(x) = 0.1 - 0.005x$. Taking the integral gives E[MAE] to be

$$\int_{r_{min}}^{r_{max}} f(x)x\,dx = \int_{r_{min}}^{r_{max}} 0.1x - 0.005x^2\,dx = \frac{r_{max} - r_{min}}{3}$$

Normalizing the MAE to the range gives NMAE=0.333, as expected.

Normal distribution Let X and Y be normally distributed random variables with mean μ and variances σ_x^2 and σ_y^2, respectively We can use the moment-generating function to model their difference [8]:

$$M_{X-Y}(t) = M_X(t)M_{-Y}(t) = e^{\frac{1}{2}\sigma_x^2 t^2 + \mu t} e^{\frac{1}{2}\sigma_y^2 t^2 - \mu t} = e^{\frac{1}{2}(\sigma_x^2 + \sigma_y^2)t^2}$$

Thus, the difference is also a normal distribution with mean 0 and variance $\sigma_x^2 + \sigma_y^2$. The density function for the MAE $|X - Y|$ is then

$$f(x) = \frac{2}{\sqrt{2\pi(\sigma_x^2 + \sigma_y^2)}} e^{-x^2/(2(\sigma_x^2 + \sigma_y^2))}$$

Fig. 6. A random art image.

Suppose $\sigma_x = \sigma_y = \sigma$. Then E[MAE] is

$$\int_0^\infty \frac{1}{\sigma\sqrt{\pi}} e^{-x^2/4\sigma^2} x\,dx = \frac{2\sigma}{\sqrt{\pi}}$$

Normalizing to the range gives an NMAE of $\frac{2\sigma}{\sqrt{\pi}(r_{max}-r_{min})}$.

Normal X, constant Y Let X be normally distributed with variance σ^2 and mean μ, and $Y = \mu$. Then the density function is exactly the standard normal distribution with mean 0 and variance σ^2, and the expected MAE is

$$\int_0^\infty \frac{2}{\sqrt{2\pi}\sigma} e^{-x^2/2\sigma^2} x\,dx = \frac{\sqrt{2}\sigma}{\sqrt{\pi}}$$

Normalizing to the range gives an NMAE of $\frac{\sqrt{2}\sigma}{\sqrt{\pi}(r_{max}-r_{min})}$. In the Jester data set, the average standard deviation is $\sigma \approx 5$, and the range is 20. Table 1 below summarizes the NMAE for different prediction models.

From Table 1, we can see that guessing the mean is almost as good a predictor as SVD. The cost of this attack is finding the mean. The adversary can do this by using a human to rate many documents, and estimating the mean from that distribution. The number of ratings needed to make a good estimate of the mean depending on the variance of the ratings. To be 90% confident that the true mean is within 3% of the sample mean in the Jester data set, the attacker would need to rate about 187 documents with $\sigma = 5$ and a range of 20:

Table 1. Normalized Mean Absolute Error (NMAE) for different prediction models.

Distribution	E[NMAE]	Jester NMAE
Uniform random	0.33	0.33
Normal	$\frac{2}{\sqrt{\pi}(r_{max}-r_{min})}\sigma$	0.28
Uniform mean	$\frac{\sqrt{2}}{\sqrt{\pi}(r_{max}-r_{min})}\sigma$	0.20
Eigentaste	—	0.187
SVD without clustering	—	0.45
SVD with clustering	—	0.34

$$n = \left(\frac{z_{\alpha/2}\sigma}{.03(r_{max} - r_{min})} \right)^2 = 187$$

This attack is simple and effective. To prevent it, a combination of a uniform distribution of ratings and better predictive algorithms is required.

7   Related Work

The ESP Game A related CAPTCHA-like scheme is the ESP Game developed at CMU [17]. The ESP Game requires two simultaneous users to label 15 images identically within 2 minutes. Moreover, there is a set of "taboo" words that both players are forbidden to use. The ESP Game is not described as a CAPTCHA. One approach to build a CAPTCHA out of the ESP Game would be to accept both players as human if they won the game.

The ESP Game is like a collaborative filtering CAPTCHA in that user data is used to grade the CAPTCHA; however, it requires online interaction, perfect matching between players, and only one other user's data is used to grade the CAPTCHA. Because the ESP Game was not designed as CAPTCHA, it is not surprising that using it as a CAPTCHA would result in a number of problems. These problems include:

– Latency. The ESP Game requires online interaction, so multiple players must simultaneously play the game. In addition, the time to take the ESP game depends on other players, who may be behind a slow network connection or malicious. A collaborative filtering CAPTCHA does not require online interaction with other human users.
– Collusion. Only two colluding players are necessary to fool the system. An adversary can automatically enter the game multiple times until she is paired with herself; then, winning the game is trivially easy. Furthermore, such an attack leads to pollution of the answer database, which is used to label images correctly in an image recognition CAPTCHA. In a collaborative filtering scheme, an adversary must work with her nearest neighbors.

– Unfairness. An adversary can automatically cause a legitimate player to lose by simply entering nonsense answers. In a collaborative filtering scheme, such an adversary would simply fail the CAPTCHA.

A more general approach to collaborative filtering CAPTCHAs sidesteps some of these problems.

Turing Game The Turing Game designed by Berman and Bruckman is one such test, though it is not a CAPTCHA because it is not automated. In the Turing game, the players are separated into the panelists and the audience [1]. The panelists pretend to be members of a particular group (such as women), and the audience of diverse gender asks questions of the panel. After the questioning, audience members vote on who is telling the truth.

SparkLife SparkLife (`community.sparknotes.com`) takes a different approach. It asks a series of fixed, multiple choice questions to determine attributes such as gender, intelligence, all-American-ness, stress level, and greed [15]. The algorithms used for analyzing the answers are not publically known.

8   Discussion

We have proposed a framework for collaborative filtering CAPTCHAs and performed a preliminary security analysis of attack models on the filter. We have shown that collaborative filtering CAPTCHAs require nearest neighbor algorithms to be useful. We have proposed a scheme for updating the collaborative filter to resist attacks and discussed security considerations for the data used in the filter.

The results of the experiments are inconclusive — however, they indicate that collaborative filtering CAPTCHAs are worthy of further investigation.

Open problems include:

– Finding an automatically renewable source of data that users can rate. Jokes must be conceived by humans, for example, but random art images are easy for machines to generate. The problem with random art images, however, is that they may not be sufficiently evocative (Section 5.3).
– Specialized collaborative filtering CAPTCHAs that are targeted at a specific demographic or group of people. Specialized knowledge could aid collaborative filtering CAPTCHAs. For example, a particular dataset (e.g., jokes) elicits different responses from different personality types or demographics. An affinity for puns might indicate linguists, or lingo-philes. A CAPTCHA based on movie data (e.g., user ratings and genre information from the MovieLens project) could target movie buffs [9].
– Using collaborative filtering to improve data sources for other CAPTCHAs. Image recognition CAPTCHAs require a human user to recognize images [2, 4, 16]. Image recognition CAPTCHAs have the problem of *mislabelling*: images in the database are indexed under meaningless labels [4].

Chew and Tygar describe CAPTCHAs requiring three tasks: naming the image by typing the label, distinguishing images, and identifying the anomalous image out of a set. Because all images are culled from Google's image database, not all of the images are labelled correctly. The mislabelling problem causes humans to fail CAPTCHAs. We can use collaborative filtering to eliminate or reduce poorly labelled images.

References

[1] Joshua Berman and Amy S. Bruckman. The Turing game: Exploring identity in an online environment. *Convergence*, 7(3):83–102, 2001.

[2] Manuel Blum, Luis A. von Ahn, John Langford, and Nick Hopper. The CAPTCHA Project. http://www.captcha.net, November 2000.

[3] Jack Breese, David Heckerman, and Carl Kadie. Empirical analysis of predictive algorithms for collaborative filtering. In *Fourteenth Conference on Uncertainty in Artificial Intelligence*, 1998.

[4] Monica Chew and J. D. Tygar. Image recognition CAPTCHAs. In *7th Annual Information Security Conference*, pages 268–279, August 2004.

[5] Chrysanthos Dellarocas. Immunizing online reputation reporting systems against unfair ratings and discriminatory behavior. In *2nd ACM Conference on Electronic Commerce*, 2000.

[6] Ken Goldberg, Robert Hennessy, Dhruv Gupta, Chris Perkins, Hiro Narita, and Mark DiGiovanni. Jester. http://shadow.ieor.berkeley.edu/humor, 1999.

[7] Ken Goldberg, Theresa Roeder, Dhruv Gupta, and Chris Perkins. Eigentaste: A constant time collaborative filtering algorithm. *Information Retrieval*, 4(2):133–151, 2001.

[8] William Mendenhall and Terry Sincich. *Statistics for Engineering and the Sciences*. Dellen Publishing Company, 3rd edition, 1992.

[9] B. Miller, I. Albert, S.K. Lam, J. Konstan, and J. Riedl. Movielens unplugged: Experiences with a recommender system on four mobile devices, 2003.

[10] Greg Mori and Jitendra Malik. Recognizing objects in adversarial clutter: Breaking a visual CAPTCHA. In *Computer Vision and Pattern Recognition*, 2003.

[11] Gabriel Moy, Nathan Jones, Curt Harkless, and Randall Potter. Distortion estimation techniques in solving visual captchas. In *Computer Vision and Pattern Recognition*, 2004.

[12] R. T. Ross. A statistic for circular scales. *Journal of Educational Psychology*, 29:384–389, 1938.

[13] J.A. Russell. A circumplex model of affect. *Journal of Personality and Social Psychology*, 39:1161–1178, 1980.

[14] Badrul Sarwar, George Karypis, Joseph Konstan, and John Riedl. Item-based collaborative filtering recommendation algorithms. In *The 10th International World Wide Web Conference*, 2001.

[15] SparkNotes. http://community.sparknotes.com, 1998–2004.

[16] Luis von Ahn, Manuel Blum, and John Langford. Telling apart humans and computers automatically. *Communications of the ACM*, 47(2):57–60, 2004.

[17] Luis von Ahn et al. The ESP game. http://www.espgame.org, 2004.

CAPTCHA Generation as a Web Service

Tim Converse

Yahoo!, CommerceNet[f]

ti□_con□erse□□ahoo□co□

Abstract. We present an implementation of CAPTCHA image generation as a REST-style web service, currently available at http://captchaservice.org. We argue that CAPTCHA generation is well suited to a web services approach, particularly one powered by open-source code, and discuss techniques for using such a service to protect weblogs from comment spam attacks.

We describe the captchservice.org API by example, and detail the workings of the two image-distortion techniques that the service offers. We also discuss accessibility objections to visual CAPTCHAs, describe our early attempts at non-visual alternatives, and summarize future development directions.

1 Motivation

In several arenas, providers and good-faith users of Internet services are at war with spammers who try to benefit by subverting those services. Email spammers send mass mailings to unwilling recipients, search-engine spammers attempt to rise in search-engine rankings by gaming search algorithms and, more recently, weblog comment spammers are exploiting the openness of weblogs to point both readers and search engines to irrelevant sites.

In all of these arenas, spam could in principle be generated as carefully as its good-faith counterparts --- the old-fashioned way, one hand-crafted chunk of spam at a time. In practice, spammers tend to deal in volume, and benefit from automation and consequent economies of scale. In some domains, then, detection of abuse can be reduced to the problem of detecting whether a human or a program is the originator.

This paper focuses on the providing CAPTCHAs and other tests of humanity as a non-profit web service, with a focus on the application of limiting automated weblog comment spam. We argue that there is particular utility in making CAPTCHA generation into a web service, and open-sourcing the code. We also discuss the interaction of CAPTCHAs and accessibility, sketch some of the opportunities and issues for CAPTCHAs that a web-service approach creates, and demonstrate some of these ideas in a REST-style web service at http://captchaservice.org/.

---

[f] □□□□ □□□□□'□ □□□□ □□□ □□□□□□□□ □□ □□□ □□□□□□ □□□□□□ □□□□□□□□□□ □□□□□ □□□□□□□□□□t□□□d □□□□ □□□□ □□□□□□□ □□ □□□s □□□□□□s □□ □ □□□□ □□□□□□□ □□□□□□□□ □□ □□□s □□□ □□ □□□□□□□□ □□ □□□□□□□□ □□□□ □□□ □□□p□□□□□N□□ □ □□□□□□4□□□i □□□ □□□□□□ □□□ □□□□□□□□□□□□ □□ ! cy 4□□□□□□L □s□□□□□□□sN- (Yy! ci

H.S. Baird and D.P. Lopresti (Eds.): HIP 2005, LNCS 3517, pp. 82–96, 2005.

1.1 CAPTCHAs and HIPs

A (AwT(HA (or Completely Automated Public Turing Test to Tell Computers and Humans Apart) is a test that verifies that the responder is a human being, by requiring evidence of an ability that is difficult to automate. (See [1] for a survey and a summary of the state of the art.) The most common CAPTCHAs in wide use are distorted images of text that are fairly easy for humans to read, yet problematic for OCR programs to decode (though see [2] for an account of breaking a visual CAPTCHA).

A note on terminology: the (AwT(HA term seems to vary widely in scope. Some restrict its meaning to tests that demonstrate humanity by reading images of distorted text, and prefer a more general term of HIP (or Human Interactive Proof) to subsume image-based CAPTCHAs as well as both non-image-based tests of humanity and other interactive tests of group membership (e.g. verification of adulthood). Others (including [1]) would call any interactive proof of humanity a CAPTCHA, as long as it also satisfies the requirement of still being difficult to break when the generation method is publicly disclosed. For the purposes of this paper, we'll use the term CAPTCHA in the narrower sense, and use the term HIP when discussing some textual challenges (that may also not pass the public-disclosure test).

1.2 Weblogs and CAPTCHAs

Weblogs (or "blogs") are on-line diaries, usually controlled by one person, but sometimes by a cooperative group. Authors typically make date-stamped entries, which are displayed in summary on a front page with most recent on top. Subject matter ranges from the extremely mundane and personal to professional, technical and political writings.

Weblogs have existed as a distinguishable web practice since at least 1999, and online journals of various kinds for much longer. In 2004, however, weblogs hit mainstream awareness in a more serious way, with thousands of new bloggers arriving every day, and with high-visibility bloggers impacting mainstream journalism, technical communities, political campaigns and political scandals.

Weblog software support has proliferated, usually taking the form either of a centrally maintained website that grants authorial privileges to bloggers (e.g. blogspot.com), or a software package that more technical bloggers who control a webserver can install and run themselves (e.g. Movable Type, Serendipity). Certain blog software features have become standard and expected: the "permalink" (a long-lasting URL that can be expected to continue to resolve to a given posting), and support for reader comments. Comments are usually follow-ups to a particular posting.

1.3 Spam and Security Needs

Weblogs with comments, then, have an ambiguous position with regard to authorial control. Typically only the author can make primary postings, and anyone (or any program) can then follow up with a comment. Comments can usually in turn include links, offering a natural incentive to abuse the system with an irrelevant comment pointing to an unrelated site. Such comment links drive traffic to the offending site either as comments are read, or via results from search engines that record the link.

Bloggers usually have an implicit community of readers in mind that they would like to empower to comment, whether it is a set of family and friends, or anyone in the world who shares a deep interest in some particular topic. Requiring that a commenter prove his or her humanity and pass a small hurdle to do so for each comment post is often an acceptable substitute (although see further discussion of this issue in the "Accessibility" section.) Note also that we are constraining ourselves to the question of who or what should have "write permission" in a given blog; for an interesting discussion of the analogous questions of read permissions and other privacy issues, see [3].

We argue not only that solving CAPTCHAs and other HIP tests are a reasonable requirement for posting a blog comment (and in fact CAPTCHA tests are now being incorporated into some popular weblog packages), but that the captcha/HIP generation process is a good candidate for abstraction as a web service, and that the code that powers such a web service is a good candidate for open sourcing.

1.4 Why a Web Service

The reasons that CAPTCHA/HIP generation makes sense as a web service are not that different from the benefits of web services in general:

o   It is a well-encapsulated task. That is, it is relatively easy to define a stable API that allows clients to request CAPTCHAs or HIPs while being insulated from the details of the algorithms that generate them.

o   CAPTCHA generation code can be written with a particular installation or library set in mind, without requiring that it run on all the platforms that the consuming software must support. This is of particular benefit when the CAPTCHA generation requires image manipulation libraries.

o   Updates to CAPTCHA generation algorithms can be deployed easily, decoupling this from more general software releases. This can be important for speed of competitive response when spammers find ways to solve particular CAPTCHA challenges.

1.5 Why Open Source

If we make the CAPTCHA-generation code freely available under an open-source license, we may reap the usual benefits of more collaborative help and more eyes finding bugs. In addition, modifiable source means that we could have different installations of the service tweaked in different ways by the server's owners. Although this sounds potentially chaotic, if multiple installations can adhere to the basic API, then client programs could pull CAPTCHAs from any of them to present to an end user, without regard to the details of how the challenge was generated.

This could in turn increase the diversity and unpredictability of the CAPTCHAs presented to automated spammers.

1.6 ☐Security Through Diversity☐

A perfect HIP would be trivial for any human to satisfy and impossible for any machine to defeat. The level of imperfection that we should settle for depends on the use case, and in particular the level of investment that makes sense for an automated attack.

For example, there may be quite a strong incentive to break a CAPTCHA test protecting account creation for a single-signon style account --- a given spammer may only need a small number of such successes to no longer need the cracking ability. By contrast, solving a CAPTCHA required for a single blog comment may not merit much in the way of resources.

The cryptographic community has long favored challenges that retain their difficulty when the challenge-generation method is open and widely known, and alternative approaches that depend on keeping the method secret are categorized dismissively as "security through obscurity". The risk of releasing CAPTCHA-generation code publicly is that you lose any security-through-obscurity benefit for the basic release. The corresponding upside is something we might call "security through diversity" --- multiple diverging installations may drive up the complexity cost for anyone hoping for a general attack. Even if there are some successes, if the success rate is low and the management headaches are high, we may help to make the spam business model less attractive.

2 A captchaservice.org Example

The CAPTCHA/HIP generation service at http://captchaservice.org is constructed using standard open-source scripting tools (PHP5 built with the gd image library) and offers a simple REST-style API. Requests are URLs with GET arguments specifying the type and optional features of the challenge/answer pair; responses are in a simple XML format, which includes both the correct answer and a presentation of the challenge. The challenge itself may be textual, in which case it is included in the XML response, or it may be an image, in which case a short-lived captchaservice.org URL for the image is included.

2.1 Server-Side Production

Here is a sample URL request to the service for an image-based captcha, with the line broken to show the GET arguments:

```
http://captchaservice.org/server.php?
   type=word_image&
   key=10
```

The 'type' argument asks for a named category of CAPTCHA, with others discussed later in the paper. (The 'key' argument is a stub to be used later for identifying requestors, should throttling become necessary.)

This request yields a response of:

```
<?xml version="1.0"?>
<captcha>
  <answer>BYWAYS</answer>
  <answertype>string</answertype>
  <challenge>http://captchaservice.com/
      imagecache/5df12ecf/8446b5bfe93e2bd6.png
  </challenge>
  <challengetype>imageurl</challengetype>
  <altchallenge></altchallenge>
  <altchallengetype></altchallengetype>
  <errorstring></errorstring>
  <errornumber>0</errornumber>
</captcha>
```

On receiving the request, the server chooses a random six-letter word, prints it to an image, distorts the image to obfuscate it writes the image to disk, and returns the XML above with the word in plain text and a URL to the stored image. (Other fields just indicate that there is no "alt" version of the challenge, and that no errors occurred.) The URL will be valid for a minimum of five minutes, but the image file will subsequently be deleted.

The corresponding PNG image shown in Figure 1 is two-color, and in this particular case was white-on-blue (although colors are controllable by the client).

Fig. 1. A CAPTCHA of the word_image type, with the random_shear obfuscation type.

Image Distortion Techniques. We currently offer two different image-distortion techniques, with the choice controllable via the client API. We refer to them here by the values that are given via that API to the 'distortiontype' GET argument: random_shear, and random_rectangles. (The 'random_shear' type is the default used when no distortiontype argument is given.)

The random_shear distortion. In the CAPTCHA shown in Figure 1, the initial image of text is distorted by randomly "shearing" it both vertically and horizontally. That is, the pixels in each column of the image are translated up or down by an amount that varies randomly yet smoothly from one column to the next. Then the same kind of translation is applied to each row of pixels (with a smaller amount of translation on average). Difficulty of the CAPTCHA can be controlled with parameters that vary the maximum amount of translation and the maximum rate of translation change (although that control is not yet exposed the client in the current implementation).

The random_rectangles distortion. Figure 2 shows what might result from a request URL like this (again, with lines broken to distinguish the GET arguments):

```
http://captchaservice.org/server.php?
    type=word_image&
    fgcolor=white&
    bgcolor=black&
    distortiontype=random_rectangles&
    key=10
```

This technique is somewhat more complicated than random_shear, and slightly more expensive.

Fig. 2. A word_image CAPTCHA with random_rectangles distortion.

First, a two-color image of text is scanned, and a list of coordinates of all pixels in the foreground color is collected. This list is randomly shuffled and then truncated at a configurable proportion of the entire list (usually about 35%), so that only a random sample of the foreground-pixel coordinates is retained. Once we have the list of coordinates, we wipe the original image clean. Finally, we iterate through this list of coordinates and draw rectangles of randomly varying sizes centered on each coordinate position.

Performance. The server-side operations performed in the CAPTCHA generation are, in order:

1. Reading a random challenge word from a disk file
2. Creating an image in internal format (gd)
3. Writing the word text onto the image
4. Obfuscating the image

5. Writing out the image to disk in PNG format
6. Creating and returning the XML wrapper for the answer and the image URL

In both distortion types we've presented, the distortion itself takes time proportional the the number of pixels in the image. As you might imagine, the most expensive step is writing out the image file. We haven't done any performance tests under load, but request-to-render time is approximately 0.25 seconds on an unloaded 1.5GHz Celeron server running Linux/Apache/PHP5. (See section 4.2 for a notes on possible performance improvements.)

2.2 Client-Side Use

In the example above, the challenge and the answer are easily extracted. A fragment of PHP5 to query the service (without error-checking) and set corresponding variables looks like this:

```
$service_url =
"http://captchaservice.org/server.php?type=word_imag
e&key=10";
$xml = simple_xml_loadfile($service_url);
$challenge_url = (string) $xml->challenge;
$answer = (string) $xml->answer;
```

If we assume that the CAPTCHA is to be used to guard a weblog comment submission, how should the client use the image and the answer? Comment submission forms can query captchaservice.org at generation time, include the URL to the newly created image in the form display, and include a text box for entry of the answer. How should the answer be retained for comparison?

One technique is for the client to save the answer and propagate it to the checking code, but (importantly) without revealing even an encrypted version of the answer on the publicly viewable form. The answer could be propagated via an associated session variable (if that capability is available in the client programming environment), or saved in a database with only the database record ID propagated to the submission handler.

Another possibility would be for the captchaservice.org server to retain the answer string in a server-side database itself, and never send the answer to client that requested the CAPTCHA. The server would support both initial requests for CAPTCHA URLs and subsequent verification requests for a yes-or-no answer about whether a supplied string was correct for a given URL. (This behavior is not yet implemented.) This invites an attack where the attacker treats the CAPTCHA server as an oracle for multiple guesses, returning to the client when a guess is confirmed. As a countermeasure, the server could insist on providing verification for any particular CAPTCHA only once, destroying the server-side information after handling a verification request. In this mode, if an attacker uses up the verification request to check a guess, that guess will then be unusable when submitted to the client.

Error Handling and Service Unavailability. The XML returned by the CAPTCHA service will generally contain both a positive error number and a diagnostic string, if for any catchable reason the generation was unsuccessful. How should client code handle errors, or the complete unavailability of the CAPTCHA server? Unfortunately, one side effect of the decoupling of the CAPTCHA generation from the client code is, of course, that the client might be functioning while the server machine is down. (In the future, clients might have a list of captchaservice installations to try in succession, but initially we'll have one server machine.)

Client code needs to have a handling policy for both explicit errors and service unavailability. In such cases, the sensitivity of the service to abuse should help determine whether unavailability of CAPTCHAs should lead to everyone being barred temporarily or everyone being admitted temporarily.

Vulnerabilities. In addition to exploitation of any clues to the answer exposed by the client, this CAPTCHA-generation method is vulnerable to a dictionary attack. By default, all the candidate words are six-letter words or proper names in English; the list of candidates used has only 6000 entries. An attacking program with access to the list, then has a 1/6000 chance of simply guessing correctly without any image analysis.

This has two implications: first, client programs should detect attempts to try guesses in bulk, most likely by tracking large numbers of incorrect guesses originating from the same IP address. Secondly, we should provide a less vulnerable generation method to those who want it. We do this by offering the CAPTCHA type random_letters_image which is identical to word_image, except that the string is composed of arbitrary letters (A-Z). (An example is shown in Figure 3.)

Fig. 3. A CAPTCHA of the random_letters_image type.

This type offers 26^6 possibilities, rather than 6000, but has less helpful redundancy for human viewers as well. (The 'L' above could as easily be a 'V', which would be less ambiguous if the string were a word.) Such random-string CAPTCHAs should probably have less extreme settings for obfuscation than word-based CAPTCHAs.

We also offer the user the alternative of supplying the challenge string (user_string_image), and simply taking advantage of the image obfuscation as a service. In this type, our resource URL looks like

```
http://captchaservice.org/server.php?
   type=word_image&
   user_string=CAPTCHA
   key=10
```

and the image returned via the URL is shown in Figure 4.

Fig. 4. A CAPTCHA created from a user-defined string.

3 Accessibility Issues

The example in the previous section does exactly what one is not supposed to do in websites that are friendly to the visually impaired: lock up crucial navigational information in an image without corresponding textual clues. Unfortunately, the opposition between CAPTCHA/HIP tests and accessibility is not trivial or easily circumvented.

The problem is that CAPTCHAs and HIPs that are designed to test for humanity do so by testing for an ability (whether sensory or cognitive), and a little bit of reflection should convince that there is no ability or combination of them that is common to every human being, or even every adult human being. Whether it's reading distorted visual images, hearing words in audio files, answering commonsense questions, or doing logic puzzles in the head --- there will inevitably be some person who lacks the requisite sense or skill, and who will therefore be locked out by the given test. (See [1] for a survey of the problem, and some proposed solutions. Unfortunately, we don't find any of the solutions particularly compelling, in that most either rely on a single-signon architecture, simply offer a solution in a different modality, or rely on social credentials that may equally inequitably distributed (e.g. possession of a credit card).)

We do not believe that this inevitability quite relieves the providers of CAPTCHAs and HIPs from worrying about accessibility. Although we believe that it is up to individual webmasters and site designers to make tradeoff decisions based on their expected audience, a CAPTCHA/HIP service should at least offer some different modalities for site designers to choose from, and ideally some multi-modal tests.

3.1 Textual HIPs at captchaservice.org

Motivated by these accessibility considerations, we've experimented with purely text-based challenges, and offer two types via the captchaservice.org site. We want to disclaim these appropriately, as they are very insecure; the generation of secure text-based captchas seems to be inherently difficult, and we are interested in any advances others have made in this area.

Odd Words Out. In the first type (odd_words_out), we present a list of words, and ask the user to indicate the word(s) that do not belong to the implicit category of the list. This can be as simple as choosing one anomalous word from a set:

jupiter
mars
mercury
clarinet
uranus
saturn
earth
venus

The generating technique here is simply to have pre-defined word sets corresponding to categories, and to present challenge sets that are predominantly drawn from one particular category.

There are two obvious vulnerabilities to this technique, the first of which is that anyone armed with the source code and the word sets could quickly write a program to detect the odd words. Secondly, even without such help, it may be easy to guess correctly by chance. In the above instance, for example, there is is one "odd" word out of eight, and so a 1/8 chance of guessing correctly.

Our initial plan for this HIP type was that we would offer, say, eight words out of which three did not belong, which would mean only a chance of 1/(8x7x6), or about 0.3% chance of guessing correctly. Our underlying assumption was that human users would solve such challenges in two steps: 1) extract the dominant theme of the list, and 2) scan the list again to locate the words that did not fit that theme. We also assumed that both steps would be easy for humans. However, we found that such challenges are annoyingly difficult. For example:

banana
tangerine
oxygen
pear
apple
horse
bassoon
orange

We suspect that most people when viewing this list would be able to arrive at the correct conclusion (i.e. that the theme of the list is fruits, and that 'oxygen', 'horse', and 'bassoon' do not belong), but the correct answer does not have the easy immediacy of the image-based CAPTCHAs presented earlier. Although we have no psychological tests to back this up, our guess is that the same combinatorics that make it hard to purely guess three odd words out of eight also make it cognitively challenging to do the first step of deriving the correct theme for a list.

Descriptions of numbers. Another non-image challenge type that we have experimented with is a textual description of a number (number_puzzle_text). Solving this HIP for a human being requires reading the text and then doing a bit of mental arithmetic to derive the desired number. An example challenge is:

the number of biological mothers a person usually has, plus one thousand

In addition to reading text and adding numbers, this asks the human reader for a little bit of commonsense reasoning to arrive at the correct answer (1001).

The generation technique here leads directly to a vulnerability. To generate these puzzles, we maintain by lists of noun phrases representing numbers, and corresponding phrases representing combining operations, including addition, multiplication, and concatenation. Each puzzle instance results from a random combination of these elements, deriving the textual phrase combination at the same time as the corresponding number. The vulnerability is that, since each puzzle is a tree-structured combination of the elements, a challenger armed with the elements themselves could write a parser to solve the puzzle. This is still considerably more difficult to automate than the odd-words-out puzzle, and could be hardened somewhat by adding a final step of textual obfuscation (say, by introducing some randomized spelling distortions). We still must note that these text-based approaches seem inherently more reversible than the image CAPTCHAs, and it is difficult to imagine them surviving a determined attack aided by access to source code. We are eager to learn about advances in this area.

Mutli-modal HIPs. Finally, we offer one genuinely multi-modal HIP, by combining the number-puzzle type with an image of the number (number_puzzle_text_image). Multi-modal or bi-modal HIPs offer the following benefits:

1) Humans with both senses or capabilities will have an easier time solving the challenge test, since they will be able to check hypotheses from one part of the challenge against the other.
2) Humans lacking only one of the capabilities will not have the benefit in OI, but will still have a chance to pass the test.
3) Programmatic attacks will most likely be reduced to trying to solve the easiest mode of challenge individually, since the cross-modal inferences in OI are notoriously difficult problems for machine intelligence.

For example, one request for a number_puzzle_text_image returned the challenge shown in Figure 5, with an "alt" challenge of "one hundred plus pi, rounded down".

Fig. 5. The visual portion of a number_puzzle_text_image CAPTCHA

4 Discussion and Future Work

We move beyond the current implementation for the moment, to discuss some general tradeoffs in CAPTCHA generation as a web service, and to explore the general problem of maintaining a consistent difficulty level in challenges.

4.1 API Design Considerations

If we assume for the moment that CAPTCHA generation is a good candidate for being an independent web service, what kinds of control would we like to offer to the requesting client?

Easy defaults and flexible controls. The most obvious desideratum is that using the simplest and most popular CAPTCHA types should be easy and straightforward to request and incorporate, with little study of documentation needed. In future versions, we plan to offer more controls and options to each type via new GET arguments, but without increasing the required arguments beyond two (the basic CAPTCHA type and an ID for the requestor for potential throttling).

Cosmetic customization. Users will inevitably want to be able to change fonts, colors, image sizes, and so on. These requests should be supported via optional arguments, with prevention of combinations that will make it impossible to solve the CAPTCHA (for example, requesting foreground and background colors that are the same, or font and image sizes that will inevitably clip the text).

Randomization. Most CAPTCHA types obviously require random choices in the generation of CAPTCHAs themselves, but the API should also provide a way to randomly vary cosmetic factors (e.g. colors) and, more interestingly, choose randomly between various CAPTCHA types. For example, client programs should be able to specify a request for randomly chosen HIP that fits a broad predefined class (say, those that present an obfuscated image where the desired answer is a string). This will allow, for example, new image transformation types to be introduced and exposed to users and bots, without any change to client code.

Difficulty control. The tradeoff between security and hassle for the human end user will be very different for different client installations; some will want just a token barrier, while others will want CAPTCHAs that could survive non-trivial automated attacks, and are willing to require substantial thought from end users. One way to support this via the API is to include a 'difficulty' argument, which can be dialed up or down for CAPTCHA types that support it. Although this is not yet implemented, it should be straightforward for the sheared-image CAPTCHAs discussed at the beginning of this paper to have difficulty levels that are mapped to image distortion parameters.

Profiles. An alternative to pre-defining classes of CAPTCHAs that might be asked for is to allow mappings from client keys to sets of control arguments, and allowing random selection between the specified types of CAPTCHAs. The profiles should be maintainable via a web interface. This should allow clients to specify sets like: "any image-based CAPTCHA of difficulty 3 or lower, with a background color of white, and a randomly varying compatible foreground color", and thereafter request the CAPTCHA by client key only. (Note that by "client" here, we mean "calling code", not "paying customer" -- we have no intention of charging money for this service.)

Configurable Obfuscation pipelines. In addition to the techniques of image obfuscation covered above, we've experimented with several others, as well as with using applying several such distortions in succession. You could imagine a client controlling the algorithm down to the level of choosing and ordering a pipeline of such modules (e.g. speckle, then shear, then blotch). Alternatively, choice of a subset and ordering of distortion modules could be a useful randomization technique.

4.2 Performance and Scaling

As discussed earlier, the captchaservice.org system has not yet encountered serious load, even in testing. It is a natural question how the system could be scaled if the service became widely used, so we note possible approaches here (although these improvements have not yet been implemented).

Clustering. The task of generating CAPTCHA images themselves could be easily spread across a cluster of servers, without any state needing to be maintained across those servers. One centralizing requirement imposed by the API is that a stable URL be returned that the client can embed in a page, but no commitments are made as to the form of that URL. You could imagine a centralized dispatching web server, that farmed requests to CAPTCHA servers in a round-robin manner, received responses in the form of server-specific pathnames, and returned the pathnames as URLs with additional encoding of the originating server. Requests for images using those URLs would be proxied to the appropriate server machine, and the image data returned to the client by the dispatching server.

Caching. A less expensive approach would be to cache some CAPTCHAs for reuse, thereby decreasing the average cost of servicing each request.

The danger here is that we do not want to provide extra information to an attacker via this caching process. For example, if we simply reuse URLs that were provided in response to earlier requests, we invite an attack where a CAPTCHA is requested and the answer and URL are saved, and then other client's pages are scanned for instances of the same URL.

Instead, it should be sufficient to reuse some image files, but generate a new file path for a symbolic link on the server to the original file. (This still invites an attack where images are requested and the full image contents are compared, but that is considerably more expensive.) In any case, the lifetime of cached images should be comparatively short.

4.3 Difficulty Control for Combinatorial CAPTCHAs

It is easy to declare an API for controlling difficulty (for humans), but designers of CAPTCHA/HIP algorithms know that it can be quite hard to achieve a consistent level of challenge across all the instances produced by a randomized algorithm. We're confident that we can map a few specified levels of difficulty to the image-shearing parameters discussed above, and that on average more extreme levels of randomized shear will correspond to greater difficulty of reading, but odd interactions of shear level and particular letters can still make for noticeable differences even with identical control parameters. The word_image type now has fairly consistent difficulty, but only as the result of careful tuning.

This problem seems to be particularly acute for combinatorial tests that gain variety by successive random choices from a set of possible elements. An example is the number_puzzle_text test discussed above, where the particular choice of operands and operators may result in substantially different mental arithmetic problems. Which of the following tests would you prefer not to do in your head?

one million times four hundred and ninety-three
eighty-four plus pi (rounded down)
type four hundred and ninety-three, and then type eighty-four immediately to the
    right of that
eighty-four multiplied by four hundred and ninety-three

We find the first three to be fairly easy, and the last to be challenging. The question is how should one design the selection of combinations like this to maintain a consistent difficulty level? Among the possible alternatives are:

- Constrain the elements and joining operators in such a way that there is no possible combination that is overly difficult. This can substantially limit the variety of the tests.
- Maintain a difficulty model that can be applied to evaluate a test at the end of generation, and repeat a random generation until you find a test with an acceptable level.

- Maintain a set of constraints on particular combinations that are invalid (e.g. no multiplication operations for operands that both have more than one significant digit), and make successive choices that respect the constraints.

We implicitly did the first of these in our first draft of the number puzzle test, and will probably do some version of the third alternative going forward.

5 Summary

We have introduced captchaservice.org, a new non-profit web service that offers a variety of CAPTCHA and HIP tests via a simple REST-style API, with an eye to use by client weblog packages. The current version offers three variants of a distorted-text CAPTCHA (presenting words, random letter strings, and user-supplied strings), two pure-text HIPs (a textual description of a number, and an "odd words out" test), and a multi-modal type combining a number puzzle with an image test. We've discussed some of the accessibility, API design, and difficulty control considerations that motivate our current and future work, and expect to continue to augment the service both with increased control via client API and with new CAPTCHA/HIP types.

6 Acknowledgements

The original idea of providing CAPTCHAs as a web service is due to Joyce Park. I have also had helpful discussions with John Wiseman, George Schlossnagle, and Sterling Hughes. This version was also improved with help from three anonymous reviewers. Thanks to CommerceNet for their support in donating and hosting the server that runs captchaservice.org, and to Joyce Park and Adam Rifkin of CommerceNet for logistical help.

References

[1] May, Brian (2003). Inaccessibility of Visually-Oriented Anti-Robot Tests, W3C Working Draft 5 November 2003. Retrieved from http://www.w3.org/TR/turingtest/.

[2] Mori, G. and Malik (2003). Recognizing Objects in Adversarial Clutter: Breaking a Visual CAPTCHA. IEEE Conference on Computer Vision and Pattern Recognition, Madison, WI, June 2003.

[3] Park, Joyce (2003). Towards Semi-Permeable Blogging. Unpublished manuscript, available at http://mod-pubsub.org/docs/semipermeable.html. To be published as a CommerceNet Technical Report.

[4] von Ahn, Luis, Manuel Blum, and John Langford (2004). Telling Humans and Computers Apart Automatically. Communications of the ACM, Vol. 47, No. 2.

Leveraging the CAPTCHA Problem

Daniel Lopresti

Department of Computer Science and Engineering
Lehigh University
Bethlehem, PA 18015
lopresti@cse.lehigh.edu

Abstract. Efforts to defend against automated attacks on e-commerce services have led to a new security protocol known as a CAPTCHA, a challenge designed to exploit gaps in the perceptual abilities between humans and machines. In this paper, we propose a new paradigm for building CAPTCHA's which offers simultaneous benefits to both online security and pattern recognition research. We illustrate our discussion with a number of examples and suggest various directions for future work.

1 Introduction

E-commerce services have become attractive targets for malicious programs masquerading as legitimate human users. Efforts to defend against such attacks have led to a family of new security protocols known as "Human Interactive Proofs," or HIP's. For our purposes, one type of HIP is of particular interest: "Completely Automatic Public Turing tests to tell Computers and Humans Apart," or CAPTCHA's. CAPTCHA challenges exploit gaps in the perceptual abilities between humans and machines. To date, most applications of this paradigm involve requiring the user to transcribe a text string that is presented in image format. Usually, the image is degraded in ways that cause no difficulty for a human user but which make the corresponding machine vision problem difficult. However, such tests can also involve recognizing a spoken utterance, solving a puzzle, etc. Having attracted the attention of an eager research community, new kinds of tasks are being proposed with increasing regularity.

CAPTCHA's, first described by Broder, *et al.* [6], have proven quite successful at preventing automated attacks. Recently, however, several well known text-based CAPTCHA's have been broken [2, 8], and it seems conceivable that others could yield soon as well. The ability to disseminate software via the Internet means that such knowledge propagates instantaneously throughout the world, posing a threat to the security of any website that depends on the compromised technology. The need to produce challenges that the general public will tolerate places constraints on how hard the tests can be, tying our hands in a sense. A critic might argue that we are witnessing an arms race that will someday be decided in favor of the crackers.

H.S. Baird and D.P. Lopresti (Eds.): HIP 2005, LNCS 3517, pp. 97–110, 2005.

Moreover, we must face the unavoidable conundrum that any CAPTCHA can be solved quickly and easily by any human user. This fact has been exploited in what has come to be known as the "pornographer-in-the-middle" attack, *i.e.*, a "bot" wishing to solve a challenge foists it off on an unsuspecting human who is, by sheer coincidence, attempting to access another, different website under the attacker's control. The operative assumption underlying most commercial CAPTCHA's – that the test consists of a single challenge to read a noisy image of a text string – appears too limiting.

While other modalities, *e.g.*, speech, are somewhat more difficult for machines, there is no reason to believe they will remain inaccessible indefinitely. Unfortunately, while current CAPTCHA solutions may lack longevity, the need to protect networked services from attack will be an ever-present problem.

In an attempt to address some of these issues, Baird and Bentley propose a family of design principles in a recent paper [1]. They observe that the act of navigating a website is a task posing inherent challenges which can be used to create a new form of "stealth" CAPTCHA utilizing tests that:

- are disguised as necessary browsing links;
- provide only a few bits of confidence, but can be answered by the user in a single mouse click aimed at the correct subregion of an image;
- require contextual knowledge to perform (*e.g.*, by labeling needed user interface "widgets" in a way that demands pattern recognition skills);
- are so easy that a single failure suggests a robot attack, at which point more stringent measures can be applied.

They argue, compellingly, that these policies result in CAPTCHA's that appear less arbitrary (and hence more appealing) to human users and that would be more difficult for machines to attack.

Building a web service that conforms to such guidelines, however, seems to require a fair amount of individualized effort and hand-tuning. New and specialized skills would probably be required of the site's designers. The ability to generate very large numbers of different challenges, cheaply, on-the-fly, and completely randomly, appears to be an open problem. If this last point cannot be resolved, such services may be susceptible to attacks where a human user proceeds through the website once recording his/her actions for later use by a bot intending to exploit it.

In any event, it is clear that a number of vexing issues remain with respect to the design, analysis, and implementation of CAPTCHA technology. The work by Baird and Bentley raises the notion that such challenges need not consist of a single pass/fail test, but can be a series of actions which, when taken as a whole, provides some level of confidence that the user is indeed human. In this paper, we build on that same general concept, but under a different paradigm and with a new, secondary goal in mind.

2   Leveraging the CAPTCHA Problem

We note with some irony that a fundamental premise behind the design of most CAPTCHA's has been that decades of research have failed to provide solutions to the pattern recognition problems in question. Yet, in a matter of months, certain types of challenges have been met in ways that are effective for the task at hand, but not particularly relevant to the original problem that motivated the CAPTCHA in the first place. Instead of helping to solve the general OCR problem for degraded text, which remains open, they can be viewed as specialized routines that are only useful for breaking CAPTCHA's. This is due to the fact that, for the most part, the challenges in question, some of which are illustrated in Figs. 1 and 2, are largely artificial, having little basis in the real world of character recognition.

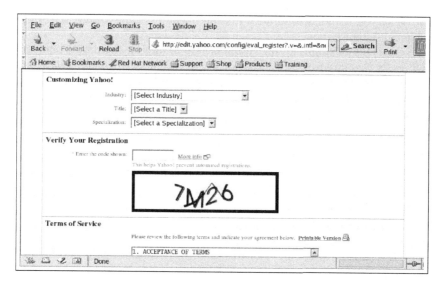

Fig. 1. The CAPTCHA protecting free Yahoo! email accounts.

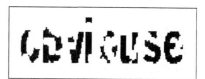

Fig. 2. Other examples of current approaches to text-based CAPTCHA's.

This observation applies not only to the effort expended to develop algorithmic techniques to circumvent CAPTCHA's, but, perhaps more significantly, to the enormous amount of time and cognitive "horsepower" exerted by the thousands or millions of human users who correctly solve the CAPTCHA's presented to them, only to have their work immediately discarded once the test is over. Although serving an important security function, the current paradigm provides no long term benefit to society beyond allowing individuals to access a protected web service.

Since substantial resources are directed towards answering CAPTCHA challenges,[1] and since nothing will deter concerted attempts to develop algorithms for attacking CAPTCHA's, we argue for a major shift in philosophy: make the use of, and even the breaking of, CAPTCHA's a "good thing." Instead of contrived questions, employ real pattern recognition tasks from important domains that are the subject of active research. Instead of discarding the input that users of a website provide, use it as ground truth labels to train and test new classifiers. Instead of prosecuting crackers who post code to break a CAPTCHA on the WWW, harvest it and incorporate it in experimental systems to solve the original problem of interest.

The benefits to adopting this viewpoint are counterbalanced by a number of open issues that need to be addressed. These include developing architectures that fuse CAPTCHA technology much more tightly with pattern recognition problems that arise in real applications. Moving away from simple tests that are tightly controlled and for which the correct answers are precisely known in advance will require rethinking the way CAPTCHA's are currently implemented. The remainder of this paper attempts to raise some of the more significant questions.

3   Community-Labeled Data: The Open Mind Initiative

A key feature of our proposal is the notion that answers to CAPTCHA challenges are too valuable a resource to be simply discarded. The problem of acquiring sufficient training and testing data to support experimental pattern recognition research is regarded as so pressing that it was one of the prime motivations behind the creation of the now-moribund Open Mind Initiative [12, 13], a project to enlist Web users in the labeling of ground-truth data for algorithm development. Whereas the incentives for participating in the original version of the project, which was modeled on the Open Source Movement, may not have been sufficiently apparent, the commercial underpinnings of the CAPTCHA problem are certainly strong enough to overcome this particular hurdle.

Our requirement that CAPTCHA's reflect real, not synthetic, tasks requires a source for such inputs. Fortunately, vast collections of multimedia data are available for this purpose, from the "in-house" training and testing data already

---

[1] A recent report notes that Yahoo!'s free email service has over 52 million subscribers, each of whom presumably had to solve a CAPTCHA along the lines of the one depicted earlier [5].

used by researchers [9] to scanned documents chosen at random from online digital libraries [7] to real-time feeds from Webcams around the Internet [15]. Instead of being limited to transcribing a simple text string, questions would reflect a particular task of interest. Some examples, taken from multimedia sources on the WWW, are shown in Figs. 3-7. Consider the fundamental difference between the nature and the usage of the data collected for the CAPTCHA shown in Fig. 2, which reflect synthetically generated images, and that shown in Fig. 4, which derives from a real letter handwritten by George Washington in the Library of Congress archive. The range of available problems – and their inherent difficulties – is at least as broad as the research programs designed to address them.[2]

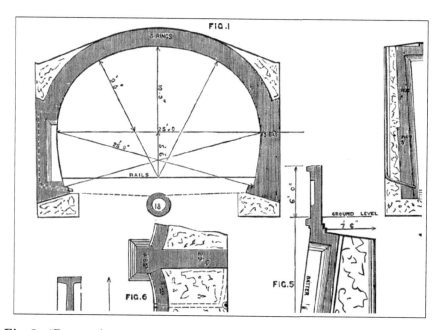

Fig. 3. "Draw a box around a text string in this image." (From the Lehigh University Library Digital Bridges project, http://bridges.lib.lehigh.edu/.)

While collecting user responses is straightforward, it may not be obvious how such a test can be used as a CAPTCHA since our assumption is that the correct answer – the vetted ground-truth – does not yet exist (otherwise there would no point in saving the user's input). Moreover, we have no guarantee that the user in question is not a machine, or that the answer he/she/it provides is correct.

---

[2] Of course, it is always possible to modify each real-world CAPTCHA slightly – *e.g.*, by re-cropping an image or injecting a small amount of noise – so that an attacker cannot assemble a collection of previously-solved tests for later use.

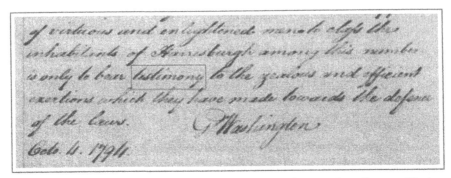

Fig. 4. "What word appears within the box?" (From the George Washington papers at the Library of Congress, http://memory.loc.gov/ammem/gwhtml/gwhome.html.)

Fig. 5. "Describe the weather in this scene." (From WABC Central Park WebCam, http://abclocal.go.com/kabc/features/cams/082102_central_Park_cam.html.)

How can such a test possibly serve as a CAPTCHA? By requiring the user to pass more than one test.

Fig. 6. "Which photos show the same person?"

Fig. 7. "How many cars do you see in this image?" (From WCPO Cincinnati Ohio Skycam, http://webcambiglook.com/cinn_skycam.html.)

Say that the user is presented with n challenges over the course of interacting with an online service, $C = \{C_1, C_2, \ldots, C_n\}$, for at least one of which, say C_i, the true response is known. Then the user's response to challenge C_i can be used to permit/deny access to the service, while the remainder of his/her responses are used to label tentatively the rest of the challenges, $C - C_i$ (assuming the user is judged to be human). Once sufficient evidence is collected to suggest that a particular answer to one of these tests is reliably known, it can enter into the set of deciding challenges. Likewise, CAPTCHA's that are found to be broken (*i.e.*, the correct response is returned by a user determined to be a machine through its failure on some other challenge) can be retired from service. Note that, as in the spirit of Baird and Bentley, it should be possible to manage the series of challenges in a way that is relatively simple and perhaps even "fun" for the user. The sequencing can also provide the context necessary to defeat the "pornographer-in-the-middle" attack described earlier since the user will have to have experienced a specific collection of tasks in a defined order to succeed.

There are numerous open questions concerning the design of such protocols. In a later section, we present one possible scenario to illustrate our ideas. Simulation studies could be an instructive way to explore this hypothesis in more detail.

4   Third Party Certification Services

A basic tenet of our proposal is that the CAPTCHA tasks must be directly connected to research questions to make ground-truth labels that are collected useful (as well as algorithms that are developed for successful attacks). It is likely that the requirements of implementing such tests will be too specialized for the average webmaster who may know little or nothing about pattern recognition research.[3] Moreover, ground-truth data is most valuable when it is amalgamated and made freely available to the research community.

There is a distinct separation between those who require the protections afforded by CAPTCHA certification for users of their website and those who provide support for the conduct of pattern recognition research. Dividing these responsibilities makes good sense. A trusted third-party authority could be established to generate and administer CAPTCHA's and certify users, much like the services provided by companies such as VeriSign Inc. [14] and RSA Security [10]. This organization would collect user responses as well as data on attempted attacks (especially successful ones) and make this information available to the pattern recognition research community in the same spirit as the Open Mind Initiative.

5   Scenario

In this section, we walk through one possible scenario to illustrate how the paradigm we are proposing might work. We observe that there are, of course, many alternatives each step of the way. For instance, while all of our examples

---

[3] Indeed, we note that there is already a significant danger of naive webmasters fielding CAPTCHA's that are too easy (and hence already breakable) without realizing it.

are drawn from a particular digital library that is freely accessible online – the George Washington papers at the Library of Congress [4] – it should be quite clear that a mixture of challenges might be more effective against certain attacks (recall Figs. 3-7). It is also important to note that new challenges are added to our system with little or no manual oversight; that is, a page is simply chosen at random from the digital library and used to create the kinds of tests we are about to describe.

Say that during the process of attempting to access a service on our hypothetical system, a user is presented with a series of five CAPTCHA challenges (Figs. 8-12). These are all related in that they reflect the common steps in ground-truthing a scanned image of a page of a handwritten document. As such, the collected data reproduce the same sorts of information present in standard datasets used for performance evaluation (e.g., [9]). It is not necessary for the individual tests to be conducted in the specified order, or even sequentially (the pages we use here are all different); other interactions may take place between CAPTCHA challenges. To obscure which tests may have been passed or failed, the final determination of whether the user is human or machine is only revealed at the end of the session, before any action requested by the user is finalized.

The first challenge, shown in Fig. 8, asks the user to identify the proper orientation for the page image (the correct answer is highlighted as if the question has already been answered). Such a weak test provides only a few bits of confidence, but, as suggested by Baird and Bentley [1], this can be sufficient when taken in the context of a series of tests. In this case, let us assume that the true answer to the CAPTCHA is not yet determined. Hence, the user's input is not distinguishing – we have no way of knowing whether it is right or wrong, whether the user is human or machine. Nevertheless, we save the response with the goal of using it to label this particular CAPTCHA if the user is ultimately judged to be human.

The second challenge is shown in Fig. 9. Here the user is asked to delimit a single text block in the page image. Say that we have already collected several inputs from users we have previously determined to be human for this particular CAPTCHA. We can use this test, then, as an indication of whether the new user is human or machine by comparing the response to the bounding boxes we believe to be correct. If it is close enough (within some predetermined threshold), we judge that the user has passed and increase our confidence in a "human" vote.

The third and fourth challenges, Figs. 10 and 11, are similar. We might assume that Fig. 10 reflects a CAPTCHA we have used on humans in the past, while Fig. 11 represents another new test we would like to add to our inventory once we have acquired sufficient evidence of the correct answer(s).

The fifth and final challenge appears in Fig. 12. Here we present a test that superficially resembles current text-based CAPTCHA's. The user is asked to transcribe the handwritten word shown on the screen (which has been segmented from the text line through its participation in an earlier CAPTCHA). Note, however, that under our paradigm, we do not necessarily know the correct text string.

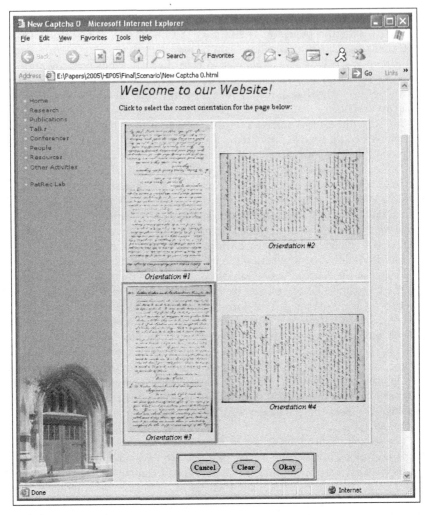

Fig. 8. "Click to select the correct orientation for the page ..."

That depends entirely on whether this test has been administered previously to one or more users determined to be human.

6   Discussion

The ideas we have put forth in this paper have several properties that make them attractive alternatives to the traditional approach to building CAPTCHA's. Although certain problems involving CAPTCHA's seem unavoidable – *e.g.*, the fact that some are breakable algorithmically and all are susceptible to indirect

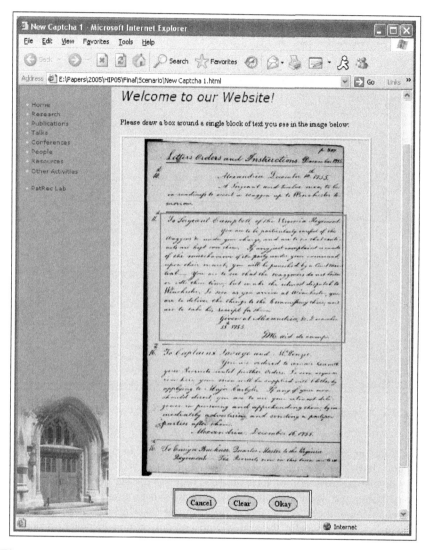

Fig. 9. "Please draw a box around a single block of text you see in the image ..."

attacks – their potential to have a positive impact on pattern recognition research would be greatly enhanced by connecting them directly to real-world problems. To date, most existing CAPTCHA's have ignored this possibility. Two notable exceptions, which do in fact derive from the field of document analysis, are Pessimal Print by Coates, *et al.* [3] and the offline handwriting CAPTCHA by Rusu and Govindaraju [11]. However, neither of these implementations was developed for the purpose of collecting labeled ground-truth data (nor, most

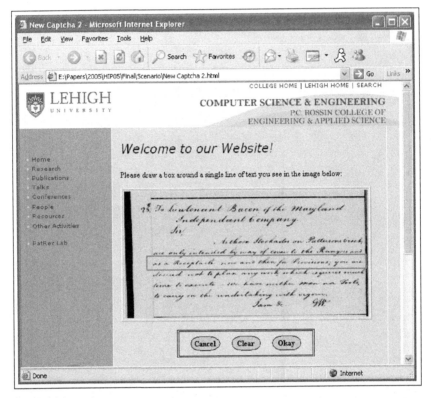

Fig. 10. "Please draw a box around a single line of text you see in the image ..."

likely, for inciting crackers to solve the true problem of interest). Indeed, both assume that the correct labels are already known.

The testing paradigm we have outlined requires further development. A number of important open questions remain. How can ground truth be used when the reliability of its labels is not yet proven? Are there attack modes that would allow a bot to overwhelm the system and not only compromise its services but also the valuable data it is collecting? Is it possible for real users (*i.e.*, humans) to become locked out if the system grows convinced that the erroneous answers provided by a certain algorithm are correct? What is an architecture that can present a coherent series of CAPTCHA challenges without, hopefully, annoying the user? These are some of the issues we hope to raise for discussion at the HIP2005 workshop.

7   Acknowledgments

We gratefully acknowledge the comments from the reviewers that helped make this a better paper.

Fig. 11. "Please draw a box around a single word you see in the image ..."

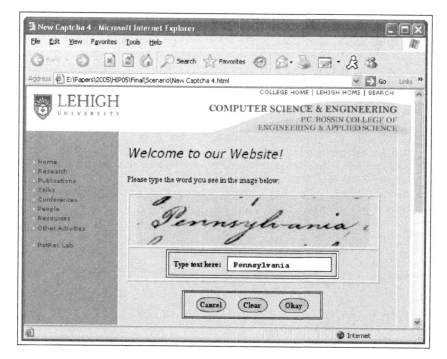

Fig. 12. "Please type the word you see in the image ..."

References

[1] H. S. Baird and J. L. Bentley. Implicit CAPTCHAs. In *Proceedings of Document Recognition and Retrieval XII (IS&T/SPIE Electronic Imaging)*, volume 5676, pages 191–196, San Jose, CA, January 2005.

[2] The CAPTCHA Project, 2004. http://www.captcha.net/.

[3] A. L. Coates, H. S. Baird, and R. Fateman. Pessimal Print: a Reverse Turing Test. In *Proceedings of the Sixth International Conference on Document Analysis and Recognition*, pages 1154–1158, Seattle, WA, September 2001.

[4] George Washington Papers at the Library of Congress, March 2005. http://memory.loc.gov/ammem/gwhtml/gwhome.html.

[5] W. Knight. Google set to sort out free email. *NewScientist.com*, April 2004. http://www.newscientist.com/article.ns?id=dn4842.

[6] M. D. Lillibridge, M. Abadi, K. Bharat, and A. Z. Broder. Method for selectively restricting access to computer systems, February 2001. U.S. Patent No. 6,195,698.

[7] D. Lopresti. Exploiting WWW resources in experimental document analysis research. In *Document Analysis Systems V*, volume 2423 of *Lecture Notes in Computer Science*, pages 532–543. Springer-Verlag, Berlin, Germany, 2002.

[8] G. Mori and J. Malik. Breaking a visual CAPTCHA, December 2003. http://www.cs.berkeley.edu/~mori/gimpy/gimpy.html.

[9] I. Phillips, S. Chen, and R. Haralick. CD-ROM document database standard. In *Proceedings of Second International Conference on Document Analysis and Recognition*, pages 478–483, Tsukuba Science City, Japan, Oct. 1993.

[10] RSA Security: solutions for enterprise data privacy and identity and access management, January 2005. http://www.rsasecurity.com/.

[11] A. Rusu and V. Govindaraju. On the challenges that handwritten text images pose to computers and new practical applications. In *Proceedings of Document Recognition and Retrieval XII (IS&T/SPIE Electronic Imaging)*, volume 5676, pages 84–91, San Jose, CA, January 2005.

[12] D. G. Stork. Character and document research in the Open Mind Initiative. In *Proceedings of the Fifth International Conference on Document Analysis and Recognition*, pages 1–12, Bangalore, India, September 1999.

[13] D. G. Stork. The Open Mind Initiative, January 2005. http://www.openmind.org/.

[14] VeriSign, Inc. – Internet and telecommunications services from VeriSign, Inc., January 2005. http://www.verisign.com/.

[15] Webcam Index – live free webcams, January 2005. http://www.webcam-index.com/.

How Much Assurance Does a PIN Provide?

Jon Bentley and Colin Mallows

Avaya Labs, 233 Mt. Airy Road, Basking Ridge, NJ 07920, USA
{jbentley, colinm}@avaya.com

Abstract. We would like to quantify the assurance contained in an authentication secret. For instance, how much assurance does a customer convey to a bank by revealing that his Personal Identification Number (PIN) is 1111? We review a number of previously proposed measures, such as Shannon Entropy and min-entropy. Although each is appropriate under some assumptions, none is robust regarding the attacker's knowledge about a nonuniform distribution. We therefore offer new measures that are more robust and useful. Uniform distributions are easy to analyze, but are rare in human memory; we therefore investigate ways to "groom" nonuniform distributions to be uniform. We describe experiments that apply the techniques to highly nonuniform distributions, such as English names.

1 Introduction

To gain access to a computer system, a user typically presents both a public name and a secret password. When the user tells that secret correctly, the system gains assurance that it really is that user, and not a lucky guesser. How much assurance is in a password? Very little if the password is "dog" (especially if a web search for the user reveals that he owns dogs), but much more if the password is "tbdam3CSQ h". Can we quantify our intuitive notion of that assurance?

Quantification would have important implications in security engineering. Current password policies are based on rules such as insisting that a password must be eight characters long, include a mixture of upper and lower case and numerics, and contain no dictionary words. We would like to quantify our intuition that "qQacwm!" is a better password than "Supercalifragilisticexpialidocious1", even though the former violates all rules and the latter is five times longer. Ideally, a security engineer would weigh assurance against cognitive effort to choose provably good password policies.

Similar issues arise in most Human Interactive Proofs. If the correct response to a CAPTCHA is "iw5r7Acq", then we feel that we have more assurance than for the string "cat". To make a quantitative statement about that example, we would have to take into account how the CAPTCHA chooses text, how the text is transformed, how the attacker recognizes characters (and what mistakes it makes), the strategy the attacker employs, and many other issues.

Most of this paper will therefore be devoted to a problem that is relatively easy to state, yet still important: how much assurance is provided by a 4-digit Personal Identi-

H.S. Baird and D.P. Lopresti (Eds.): HIP 2005, LNCS 3517, pp. 111–126, 2005.
© Springer-Verlag Berlin Heidelberg 2005

fication Number (PIN)? Extensions to more subtle problems are examined in later sections.

2 The Technical □uestion

To use an Automated Teller Machine (ATM), a customer needs both a bank card and the corresponding 4-digit PIN. If the card is lost or stolen, the PIN provides some protection against its unauthorized use by an attacker. How can we measure the amount of protection the PIN affords?

We take as axiomatic that the degree of protection, which we call assurance, is measured by the probability p that an attacker can guess the PIN. We find it convenient to speak of the number of bits[1] of assurance, which is $-\log_2 p$ (all further logarithms in this paper are base 2). We write $assurance((\; \mathcal{Q}) = -\log w((\; \mathcal{Q})$, where $w((\; \mathcal{Q})$ is the probability that an attacker A guesses the customer $($'s PIN correctly. The bank may feel that by implementing a 4-digit system, they have provided each customer with $\log 10000 \; \mathcal{Q} 13.3$ bits of assurance. But can a particular customer, who may have chosen as his PIN the easy-to-remember number 1111, have this degree of assurance? And what about a sophisticated attacker, who has found a bank card, and knows a lot about how people choose PINs?[2]

We do not have access to large sets of real PINs for real ATM cards, so we did several simple experiments to study the PINs that people use in other domains. A web search for "passwords name pin cheats" gave a variety of web sites that list "cheat codes" for computer and video games, many of which require a 4-digit PIN. The web site www.gamefaqs.com/computer/doswin/code/25003.html, for instance, gives this set of 41 PINs, which we present in sorted order:

> 0201 0310 0322 0425 0517 0526 0530 0604 0818 1029 1111 1111
> 1111 1111 1111 1111 1112 1122 1221 1234 1836 2220 3141 3246
> 3333 3333 3333 3691 4288 4393 4440 5158 5651 6000 6660 6765
> 6969 7761 7777 8148 8337

The authors feel confident in asserting that a uniform random process did not generate those 41 PINs. Six of the numbers are 1111; an attacker who guesses that PIN has about a 15% chance of success, which indicates under 3 bits of assurance. Four other PINs also contain a single digit. The PINs 1112, 2220, 4440, 6000 and 6660 deviate in just a single affix digit. Of the numbers that begin with the digit pair 00 through 12, all but 1234 have second digit pairs less than 31, which make us think of dates (birthdays seem particularly likely). Excluding these PINs leaves us with less than a third of the original set:

---

[1] Shannon [1948] begins by counting the number of messages, and quickly moves to the logarithmic measure of bits. We find the logarithmic measure more appropriate for assurance for the same three reasons that Shannon found the logarithmic measure more appropriate for information: it is more useful, nearer intuition, and more mathematically suitable.

[2] A bank may allow a customer several attempts at entering a PIN, to allow for mistyping and the like. If the attacker fails on his first attempt, he should simply ignore that PIN and proceed with the next-best possibility. For simplicity, we ignore this complication, and assume that only one attempt can be made.

1836 3141 3246 3691 4288 4393 5158 5651 6765 6969 7761 8148 8337

Even this subset does not appear to have been chosen at random; only three of the thirteen PINs have four different digits, though more than half of the 10000 possible PINs have that property.

This simple experiment is not atypical. At another site, 14 of 34 players used the PIN 1111. One of the authors is willing to admit that at one time, one of the three ATM cards in his wallet had the (default) PIN 1111 (that card is now discarded). Such experiments and decades of bitter experience (see Morris and Thompson [1979]) lead to our basic assumption:

Humans tend to choose secrets in nonrandom and repeated patterns.

3 Assurance Is Not Entropy

We might assume that a 4-decimal-digit keyspace of PINs means that an individual PIN yields about 13.3 bits of assurance. But if many users choose the PIN 1111, then that particular PIN should carry fewer bits of assurance. How can we quantify that intuition? Many information scientists (including the authors and several of their colleagues) jump to the answer, "Entropy, of course!" That answer is wrong.

One approach to authentication is to ask people questions that are easy to remember yet are hard for attackers to guess (see O'Gorman, Bagga and Bentley [2004]). Such a question with four answers can be viewed as a 2-bit PIN. Our internal corporate web site offers a daily straw poll with questions such as "What is your favorite way to celebrate a holiday?" The answers and their (rough) percentages are

Gather with family and friends	71%
Catch up on chores	17%
Attend a wild party	11%
Volunteer at a shelter	1%

The maximum possible entropy for four answers is 2 bits (when each occurs uniformly, 25% of the time). Interpreting the percentages as probabilities gives an entropy for these nonuniform answers of 1.2 bits. On the other hand, an attacker who guesses "family and friends" has a 71% chance of being right on this question, and slightly more than a 50% chance of being right on two such questions in a row. Our intuition says that such an answer should therefore be worth at most half a bit of assurance. Evidently, assurance is not entropy.

Shannon [1949] first examined related issues in terms of "secrecy systems". A great deal of work has been done since then in "authentication theory". Cachin [1997, Section 3.1] surveys information measures that have been used in cryptography to characterize probability vector $p = (p_1, p_2, ..., p_N)$, where the probabilities have been ordered so that $p_1 \geq p_2 \geq ... \geq p_N$. He starts by reviewing the classical Shannon entropy of $-\Sigma_i\, p_i \log p_i$. He also describes the min-entropy of $-\log p_1$, which characterizes the probability of guessing the most likely element, and therefore the largest security hole (such as "family and friends" above). The guessing entropy $\Sigma_i\, i\, p_i$ gives the expected cost of a sequential search (Knuth [1973, Section 6.1]) for a secret, starting at the most likely guess and progressing until the answer is found. This measure might describe the time required to guess a hashed password, given a dictionary of all passwords ordered by frequency. Other measures that Cachin describes include *relative entropy, - enyi entropy of order* α, *collision probability*, and *variational distance*. None of these measures, though, directly addresses the issue of concern to us: how much assurance is in a particular secret? (Though we will see in the next section that many of these measures are very relevant in particular contexts.)

In his "Unified and generalized treatment of authentication theory", Mauer [1996] cautions us that "Compared to the theory of secrecy, authentication theory is more subtle and involved." Ellison, Hall, Milbert and Schneier [1999] point out that "Research needs to be done on the actual entropy (from the attacker's point of view) of a given class of answers...." With that warning and challenge, we now address those issues.

4 Three Views of Nonuniform Probabilities

Three players are in the game. The first is the Bank, B, which chooses N, the size of the key-space (N=10000 for a 4-digit PIN). The second is the customer, $($, who chooses a particular PIN $\Box(($), and who is interested in the probability that this particular PIN can be guessed. The third is the attacker, A, who (we assume) may know everything about the key system, except the value of the particular PIN that goes with the bank card he has found.[3] In particular, we assume that the attacker may have access to statistical information regarding the frequencies of the various PINs.

Each of these players has different concerns. The customer is interested in the degree of protection afforded by his own PIN. The bank is interested in one or more summary statistics regarding its customers, for example the average degree of protection they have, or the protection given to the least-protected customer. The attacker is interested in the probability that he will be able to guess the PIN associated with the particular bank card he has found, which we assume is randomly chosen from all the bank customers.

4.1 The Attacker

It is convenient to start with the attacker. A naïve attacker will guess all possible values of $\Box(($) equally often, with the chance of success of precisely $1/N$. The bank therefore achieves $\log N$ bits of assurance against that attacker, which we will refer to as the *ma$\Box$entropy* (by analogy with min-entropy). At the other extreme, a well-informed attacker might know the probability vector $p = (p_1, p_2, ..., p_N)$, which gives the probabilities with which each of the N possible PINs is used. We suppose the possible PINs have been ordered so that $p_1 \geq p_2 \geq ... \geq p_N$. Now suppose that $p_1 = p_2 = ... = p_k > p_{k+1}$. Then the attacker's optimal strategy is to guess one of $\Box_1, \Box_2, ... , \Box_k$, and (whether or not he randomizes among these possibilities) $w((\Box)$ is just p_1. Any

---

[3] The Attacker (A), Bank (B) and Customer ($($) of authentication collectively apologize to Alice (A), Bob (B), and Carol ($($) of cryptography for unintentional identity theft.

other strategy will decrease $w((\ Q)$. In this case, the min-entropy accurately charac-terizes the weakest link in the chain.

In the first case, the attacker has information about no PINs, while in the second case, he knows the distribution of all PINs. To define a state of knowledge interme-diate between these two, we consider an attacker who has access to a single random PIN, say y, chosen from all the PINs of the bank's customers. The optimal strategy for this "single-peek" attacker is to guess $\Gamma(\ ) = y$, and his chance of success on this occasion is p_y. The overall chance of success for an attacker of this type is $w_A = \Sigma_y (p_y)^2$ (because it is the probability that the customer's choice of PIN matches the one the attacker has seen). We have $1/N \le w_A \le p_1$, so the assurance is between the max-entropy and the min-entropy. Furthermore, the weighted average assurance of a cus-tomer with respect to this single-peek attack is the Shannon entropy $-\Sigma_i p_i \log p_i$.

One can consider the more general case of an attacker who has a sample of size m of the PINs; the previous results are special cases for $m = 0$, 1, and ∞. Bentley and Mallows [2005] prove that w_A is in fact a non-decreasing function of the size of the sample.

4.2 The Customer

Now consider a customer C with a particular PIN, $\Gamma(\ )$. This customer wants to know the probability that an attacker will guess exactly this PIN. If the correspond-ing p is not equal to p_1, we could argue that this customer is perfectly protected, since an optimal attacker with complete knowledge will never guess this PIN. But what about an attacker who chooses a different strategy? To measure the degree of assur-ance the customer has, we need to be specific as to what attacks are considered. Clearly, there is no protection against an attacker who has inside information as to this particular PIN. We assume that the most an attacker can know is statistical in-formation as to the distribution of PINs over the bank's customers, that is, the com-plete vector p. We cannot allow the possibility that an attacker may have any possi-ble (mistaken) value of p, since this would allow the possibility that he believes that the particular PIN $\Gamma(\ )$ is very likely. We need to specify the information the attacker may have, ranging from none to complete (accurate) knowledge of p.

A naive attacker will guess $\Gamma(\ )$ correctly with probability $1/N$, no matter what p is. An attacker who has seen a single PIN, say y, and who guesses that value for $\Gamma(\ )$ will succeed with probability p_y. An attacker who knows p completely, and who therefore guesses some y with $p_y = p_1$, can succeed (in guessing $\Gamma(\ )$) only when $p = p_1$ and otherwise is sure to fail. We suggest that an appropriate measure of the assur-ance that a customer $($ has is the minimum of these three values, so that

$$assurance(\mathrm{x}) \ = \ - \log \max(1/N, \ p) \tag{1}$$

Note that this conservative formula is correct both when $p = p_1$ and when $p \ne p_1$.

The formula (1) is not completely satisfactory. Consider a key-space with $N=5$, and two alternative p-vectors: $p^a = (.4, .3, .1, .1, .1)$ and $p^b = (.3, .2, .2, .2, .1)$. Ac-cording to (1), the PINs with $p = .3$ are equally secure in these two cases, but this seems wrong since an attacker who knows p (or even an approximate value of p) will guess this PIN correctly in case (b) but will never do so in case (a). More appropriate measures of assurance might take rank into account.

4.3 The Bank

While a naive view is that a 4-digit PIN affords the max-entropy of log 10000 Q 13.3 bits of assurance, the bank cannot claim that each individual customer has this degree of assurance. More relevant measures include the mean assurance (the Shannon entropy, for a single-peek attacker) and the assurance given the most vulnerable customer (the min-entropy). The bank can improve these measures in several ways. One way, which is done by few banks and resented by many customers, is to issue random PINs to customers instead of allowing customers to choose their own PINs. But even this approach raises difficult questions: What if current customers have typical PINs, and a random process issues a new customer the common PIN 1111?

Alternatively, the bank can urge its customers to avoid "common" PINs, but how can this be done without giving away information as to which PINs are common? One possibility is for the bank to urge its customers to choose PINs that contain four different digits. This reduces the key-space to N = 5040, and so surrenders about one bit of assurance relative to the full N=10000. Yan, Blackwell, Anderson and Grant [2000] apply such an approach to computer passwords.

4.4 Who □nows What When□

We have seen that assurance depends strongly on what the attacker knows about the distribution of the PINs. If the attacker assumes that each element is equally likely, then the assurance is the max-entropy of log N bits; if the attacker knows the most likely key, then the assurance is the min-entropy of $-\log p_1$ bits; if the attacker samples a single key, then the weighted average assurance is the Shannon entropy.

The attacker's strategy can also change as a function of what he knows (or assumes) about the assurance that the bank assigns to each guess. If an attacker knows the complete probability distribution, and also knows that the bank assigns the same assurance to every correct answer, then his optimal strategy is to choose the most likely PIN. But if the bank knows that that attacker will behave in exactly that way, then the bank should assign small assurance to the most likely answer. In fact, if the bank assumes that the knowledgeable, rational attacker makes that choice with probability 1, then it must associate $-\log 1 = 0$ bits of assurance with that answer, and infinite assurance with every other answer.

But if the attacker in turn knows that the bank employs that modified policy, then the attacker's revised optimal strategy is to choose the second most frequent PIN. And so it goes, depending on who knows what when. After wandering through a game-theoretic analysis reminiscent of "Rock-Paper-Scissors", we soon arrive at "The Paradox of the Surprise Examination" (see Wischik [1996]).[4]

---

[4] In that paradox, the teacher announces to a class that there will be an exam one day next week (Monday through Friday) on a day when the students do not expect it. But the exam cannot

Many analyses show such a lack of stability. The bank posits a set of probabilities and assurances, and analyzes the attacker's strategy, which results in a new and distinct set of assurances. A stable strategy always exists in a two-person, zero-sum game. Unfortunately, we do not see how to formulate the present problem as such a game. We will study an alternate approach to stability in the next section.

5 Inducing Uniformity

Analysis of uniform probabilities is straightforward. Unfortunately, few events in human memory are truly uniform; humans tend to know obscure but nonuniform facts. In this section we will study ways in which we can induce uniformity.

5.1 Accumulating Assurance

So far we have considered the assurance of a single transaction: how much does one answer yield? In many contexts, though, we are interested in accumulating the assurance of a sequence of questions. To gain access to personal financial information, for instance, one has to give correct answers to a series of questions such as "what is your birth date?" and "what are the last four digits of your Social Security number?" We now turn our attention to systems that collect a large number of questions and answers from a user at registration, and at login ask a subset of the questions to authenticate the user in the presence of potential attackers.

The probability that an attacker correctly guesses one of 16 items chosen uniformly is 1/16, which corresponds to 4 bits of assurance. If the bank presents a second independent question of 16 choices, then the probability and bits are the same. The probability of correctly guessing both answers multiplies to 1/256, and the bits correctly sum to 8. Straightforward accumulation of assurance is indeed straightforward.

Accumulation becomes subtle when the attacker knows more about the bank's mechanism. If the attacker has guessed enough correct answers to need just one more bit of assurance to break in to an account, for instance, then he might take a very different approach than when he still needs to accumulate many bits, and this can substantially change the attacker's optimal strategy. The change in strategy can change probabilities, which also changes bits of assurance. Henceforth we will ignore this complication, and assume that the attacker's goal is to act for the long run.

5.2 Grooming a Single ☐uestion

Perfectly uniform distributions are hard to attack, easy to analyze, and, unfortunately, relatively uncommon in human memories. Even gender is not determined by a fair

---

take place on Friday, because after Thursday had passed with no exam, the students would expect it on Friday. For the same reason, the exam could not take place on Thursday, and so on.

coin toss -- the (*IA World Factbook* (at www.cia.gov/cia/publications/factbook/) reports that at birth the male/female ratio in the USA is 1.05. But just as dieters hope that "inside every fat person is a thin person trying to get out", so we observe that "inside every skewed distribution is a uniform distribution trying to get out".

To induce uniformity into a nonuniform binary question, for instance, we can randomly exclude some members of the larger set. For example, assume that 1000 registrants report that their gender is female, and 1050 report male. An attacker might gain a slight advantage by guessing male more often than female. We can remove that advantage by randomly selecting 50 of the males to exclude from that question; we instead use other questions to verify their identity. The result is a perfectly balanced question, which provides precisely one bit of assurance.

For a multiple-choice question, assume that 1000 responses to a four-answer question occur with these nonuniform frequencies:

A	B	C	D
350	325	300	25

We can *groom* this into a perfectly uniform question for 900 of the respondents by excluding all 25 Ds and randomly excluding 50 As and 25Bs:

A	B	C
300	300	300

We have chosen answer C as the *grooming point*. We will no longer ask this question of the 100 excluded respondents (50 As, 25 Bs and 25 Ds), and instead ask other authentication questions of them. (In this single-question grooming, it is important to exclude the respondents before any login attempts; if we randomize at each login, an attacker might observe that a certain question is asked rarely, and thereby deduce that the particular respondent gave a common answer.) We have induced perfect uniformity by trimming ten percent of the responses, at the cost of reducing the number of bits of assurance per response from the maximum possible of 2 to just log 3 Q 1.585. If a knowledgeable attacker does not know that the distribution has been groomed, he might still tend to answer A; his probability of success is exactly 1/3, which is accurately reflected in the bits of assurance.

The grooming process divides a distribution into three parts:

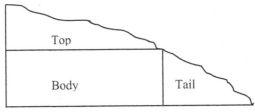

The grooming point is the right boundary of the Body, and the height of that particular value defines the top of the Body. The elements in the Top are discarded at random; the elements in the Tail are all discarded, and the result is the uniform Body. Those remaining elements are truly uniform. If the grooming point is at the Mth element, then log M bits of assurance are assigned, and the probability of an attacker guessing a randomly chosen element on the first try is $1/M$, and by the $+^{th}$ try is $+/M$, the expected number of guesses before success is $(M+1)/2$, and the worst-case number is M. It is not coincidental that after grooming, we have the condition $p_1 = p_2 =... = p_M > p_{M+1} \geq ... \geq p_N$ that we analyzed in Section 4.1.

We have extended the basic idea of grooming in several ways. We can admit the elements in the Tail (the 25 people who answered D above, for instance) without compromise by still assigning just log M bits for each answer. This conservative policy provides a lower bound on the number of assurance bits and therefore an upper bound on the probability of an attacker successfully guessing.

In the example above, answer C was an obvious grooming point. Grooming to answer D would have reduced all counts to 25, and therefore excluded too many answers. Grooming only to answer B would have raised one count from 300 to 325, but at the cost of reducing the bits of assurance from log 3 to log 2. A linear-time program can scan a sorted sequence of frequencies (or probabilities). If registration time is critical, then one might choose the grooming point as the item that maximizes the number of bits per response times the number of non-excluded responses, which is the bits per original response. If login time is critical, then one might choose a larger grooming point to collect more bits at each authentication attempt.

The table below shows the effect of grooming point. The first four columns give the percentages of a population (in nonincreasing order), and the last three columns present the bits per original response for the three grooming points. The first three rows give uniform distributions (over 4, 3 and 2 answers), the fourth row gives the example we used earlier in this section, and the next seven rows give real distributions from the straw poll referred to in Section 3. Because the first row describes a uniform distribution, the right entries give the max-entropy. The 8th line in the table shows that bits per original response is not unimodal in the grooming point. Section 6.1 describes grooming larger data sets.

wercentages				Mrooming woint		
				2	3	4
25	25	25	25	1	1.58	2
33.3	33.3	33.3		1	1.58	
50	50			1		
35	32.5	30	2.5	0.98	1.47	0.20
31.3	30.9	20.6	17.2	1.00	1.25	1.37
34.5	34.4	16.0	15.1	1.00	1.00	1.21
38.6	32.7	20.5	8.3	0.94	1.10	0.66
40.7	35.4	12.7	11.2	0.95	0.78	0.89
63.2	26.1	6.6	4.2	0.63	0.38	0.33
63.6	18.3	10.8	7.3	0.55	0.63	0.58
65.7	17.0	9.8	7.5	0.51	0.59	0.60

Some pairs of questions that are singly well suited for authentication have the disadvantage of being statistically correlated. At an extreme, the questions of state of birth (with the answers Hawaii and Minnesota) and favorite childhood sport (with the answers surfing and ice hockey) likely show a strong correlation. Once an attacker guesses one answer to a question, he should be constrained about further guesses.

We can incorporate this fact into the analyses of Section 4 by using conditional probabilities.

Alternatively, we can remove the need for conditional probabilities by pairwise grooming to induce independence. Suppose that two potential authentication questions ask of voters in the 2004 USA presidential election "With what party are your registered?" and "For whom did you vote for president?" Further assume that in one (illustrative, not typical) community, 1000 respondents had this matrix of answers:

	Republican	Democrat
Bush	300	200
Kerry	200	300

That is, 300 Republicans voted for Bush and 200 Republicans voted for Kerry, while the Democrats voted in exactly the opposite numbers. We can replace that matrix with the uniform 2×2 matrix that consists of four entries of 200 by randomly grooming out 100 of the 300 Republican Bush voters and 100 of the 300 Democratic Kerry voters.

5.3   Grooming a Series of ⬚uestions

Suppose that the bank has recorded the answers that each customer has given to a large set of questions. We assume that an attacker knows the frequency with which each answer is given in the population of customers, but does not know anything about the particular customer he is attacking. To assess an attack, the bank needs to choose some set of questions to ask, such that the probability that the attacker succeeds in answering all these questions correctly is less than some preassigned value.

This objective can be achieved in the following way, at least when all questions have the same number of answers. Suppose the responses to each question have been ordered from most popular to least popular. The bank chooses a sequence of M desired responses as a sequence of independent random variables having some common distribution F, which the bank chooses; the attacker may know F. The bank then asks questions that this particular customer has answered in the desired way. From the attacker's point of view, he is trying to guess a sequence of independent random variables, distributed according to F, so his optimal strategy is to give the most likely response (according to F) every time. The fact that he can observe which questions are being asked does not help him. (This remark is not entirely trivial.) The probability that the attack succeeds is just f_1^M where f_1 is the largest probability in F.

This scheme cannot be applied to protect a customer who has not given a sufficiently diverse set of responses.

While this scheme does provide the customer with the desired measure of assurance, a customer who is successfully attacked may feel cheated because although he answered many questions with responses other than the most popular one, on this occasion the (incompetent) bank asked only questions that were easy to guess. To avoid this outcome, let us change the bank's strategy. The bank can work out how many realizations of each possible response can be expected in M questions; it constrains the sequence of desired responses so that it is a random permutation of these numbers of each response. The bank announces this information, so an attacker who has been paying attention will now choose his guesses in the same way: as a random permutation of these numbers of each type of response. The probability that the attacker succeeds is now the reciprocal of a multinomial coefficient. Any other attack has a smaller chance of succeeding. The bank can therefore design the scheme to provide any desired degree of assurance.

6 Applications

So far we have described our techniques in straightforward contexts. In this section, we will see how the methods can be applied in more substantial domains.

6.1 Names

Many humans are able to remember the names of childhood friends, and that information is often difficult for attackers to learn (at least it was before membership in youth clubs was posted on the Web). How much assurance is contained in a name such as Mary or Ardelia or Smith or Aalderink? We will study data from the U.S. Census Bureau's web site at www.census.gov/genealogy/www/freqnames.html. A file of 88,799 last (family) names accounts for 90% of the sample population and begins with these three lines:

```
SMITH           1.006   1.006       1
JOHNSON         0.810   1.816       2
WILLIAMS        0.699   2.515       3
```

The names appear in decreasing order by frequency. The second line says that the name Johnson accounts for 0.810 percent of the sample population, that the names so far in the file account for 1.816 percent, and that Johnson is the second most frequent name in the sample. The min-entropy is $-\log 0.01006 = 6.635$ bits for Smith. The Shannon entropy of that file is 9.969 bits, which is the weighted average assurance (over all customers) against a single-peek attacker.

We wrote a linear-time program to groom the set of names, and found that the grooming point that maximizes total assurance bits was at Adkins, the 394th name in the file, which accounts for 0.029 percent of the names. All names are therefore assigned $\log 394 = 8.622$ bits of assurance. The 394 names account for 32.478% of all names, but we must exclude some fraction of those (that occur above the threshold of 0.029%). For instance, we exclude the unlucky 0.670% of the population that had the last name of Williams and was chosen to be excluded by grooming; we also exclude half of the people named Dunn (the 160th most common name, with 0.058% of the sample). Altogether, grooming excludes 21.448% of the population, but assigns 8.622 bits of assurance to the remaining 78.552% of the population. That gives an average of 6.807 bits per (original) name.

The probability of success of any attacker against a randomly chosen name is at most 1/394. Still, the few Smiths lucky enough to survive grooming might feel that they are particularly vulnerable against an attacker who is knowledgeable about the distribution of last names yet ignorant of the fact of grooming. The Bank could soothe those fears by announcing to all potential Attackers that the data had been groomed.

We applied similar analyses to files of male and female first names from the same web site. (Since the popularity of first names changes quickly over the years, a clever attacker should take birth date into account, and use names popular at the time.) The 1219 male names accounted for 90% of the population, with Qames the most popular at 3.318%. The optimal grooming point was at the 77th name (Aaron, which accounted for 0.240% of all names). This assigned log 77 = 6.267 bits of assurance to the non-excluded 63.77% of the population, for an average of 3.997 bits per (original) name. The 4275 female names accounted for 90% of the population, with Mary the most popular at 2.629%. The optimal grooming point was at the 112th name (Rosa, which accounted for 0.194% of all names). This assigned log 112 = 6.807 bits of assurance to the non-excluded 76.24% of the population, for an average of 5.190 bits per (original) name. Our experiments are summarized in this table.

	Total Names	Shannon Entropy	Min-Entropy	Mrooming woint	Bits wer Name	Names E⬗ cluded	Bits wer Yriginal Name
Last	88,799	9.969	6.635	394	8.622	21.45%	6.807
Female	4275	8.591	5.249	112	6.807	23.76%	5.190
Male	1219	7.386	4.914	77	6.267	36.23%	3.997

6.2 Grooming PINs

Grooming is straightforward to apply to multiple-choice questions in which there are a handful of options. Grooming is also useful for four-digit PINs. Suppose, for instance, that of the 10,000 possible four-digit PINs, 8000 were rarely chosen, while 2000 were chosen frequently. We would choose a grooming point of 2000 in the descending-frequency list of PINs, and therefore conservatively assign just log 2000 (or about 11) bits of assurance to each PIN. We would still ask about the 8000 PINs in the Tail, but we would not use them to compute assurance.

Let us further suppose that of the 2000 frequent PINs, most were chosen relatively uniformly, while a popular few were chosen often (such as 1111, 1234, 9876 and the like). We might coerce the users to change them those particularly common PINs, or insist on some additional information at authentication. Alternatively, we could assign less assurance, using formula (1) from Section 4.2. The small assurance might be enough to inquire about account balance, for example, but not enough to drain money from an account.

6.3 How Much Assurance Does a CAPTCHA Provide⬚

In a Completely Automated Public Test to tell Computers and Humans Apart (CAPTCHA), the Bank wishes to distinguish a human Customer from a robotic Attacker. Rather than providing each human a distinct secret password, the bank gives a test that is easy for humans yet hard for computers. A typical test is to read a sequence of distorted letters. The test should provide little inconvenience to a human, but enough difficulty so that an attacker usually fails the test. Assurance is an appropriate measure of that difficulty.

How well does a blind Attacker do against a CAPTCHA of visual letters? If the challenge text is chosen uniformly from a dictionary of 1024 common words, it carries 10 bits of assurance (the randomly guessing Attacker has probability $1/1024$ of success). If 8 characters are chosen uniformly from a set of 32 characters (start with 26 upper-case letters and 10 digits, and throw out near misses like "I" and "1" and "2" and "Z"), then the text will have $8'5 = 40$ bits of assurance. When Chew and Baird [2003] generate a pronounceable 8-character challenge from an order-3 Markov chain, how many bits of assurance does it carry? While the exact probability of the process selecting the given challenge is straightforward to compute, we conjecture that the inherent nonuniformity will make the probability of a clever attacker succeeding in guessing very hard to determine. We also conjecture that a "groomed" Markov chain would be easy to analyze yet still yield challenges that "look like" English text.

Smart attackers of CAPTCHAs use Optical Character Recognition systems that are far from blind. How do we analyze their probability of success? We conjecture that a misrecognition matrix showing how often each character is mistaken for another ("C" might be mistaken for "O" more frequently than it is for "X") will be key for such analysis.

6.4 Lotteries

Consider a lottery where patrons choose a key (from some known finite set) and winners are decided by a random draw (perhaps on TV using a physical randomizing mechanism). This is an instance of a special case of our problem where the Attackers are the patrons, and the secret password is the randomly selected winning key. It differs from our general case in that there is no analog of the particular Customer, who owns an individual password and has an interest in its security. For such a uniform lottery, both the bank and the patrons can agree that the security of the key is properly measured by the size of the key-space (or the logarithm of this).

Now suppose that the randomizing mechanism does not produce keys uniformly. (This happened in the early days of the US draft lottery.) We assume that successive draws are independent, but not uniformly distributed. If the true distribution is not known by the patrons, they will still measure security by $\log N$, and will have no reason to prefer one key over another. If they do know the distribution, however, or if they get an estimate of it by accumulating data over time, then they will need to reassess. The system becomes all the more interesting if the winnings are divided equally among fellow successful attackers, so attackers benefit from selecting an answer that is guessed by few other attackers. Becker, Chambers and Wilks [1988, Section 1.2] describe how this happened early in the New Qersey Pick-It Lottery.

7 Conclusions

Dictionaries define assurance as a statement that inspires confidence. The goal of this paper is to quantify the amount of assurance contained in a particular message. In Human Interactive Proofs, that message might be the answer to a multiple-choice question, a PIN, the text in a visual CAPTCHA, or a password.

Section 2 phrases the problem in terms of PINs, and gives anecdotal evidence to show that human secrets tend to be nonrandom. Section 3 shows that neither the classical Shannon entropy nor other more recent entropic proposals completely captures assurance.

Section 4 surveys ways of quantifying assurance from various viewpoints. Many of the modifications of entropy are in fact relevant in various contexts. For nonuniform distributions, though, the assurance varies greatly with assumptions regarding the knowledge of the attacker and regarding "who knows what when". Section 5 therefore proposes methods to "groom" nonuniform distributions to induce uniformity. By guaranteeing uniformity we ensure that we can employ the straightforward measure of max-entropy. Section 6 shows how the methods can be applied to problems in and beyond human authentication.

This paper has taken steps towards a theory of assurance. Our long-term goal, though, is assurance engineering, which would allow authentication engineers to quantify the assurance of various schemes. In designing a CAPTCHA, for instance, we might want to know how much assurance is contained in 10-characters of order-4 Markov text versus 6 characters of order-1 Markov text. We could use such numbers together with analyses of readability, pronouncability, familiarity and so forth to achieve a provably good design. We consider the following problems particularly ripe for further work.

Improvements to Mrooming. Section 5 described straightforward grooming algorithms, and Section 6 showed that they are fairly efficient in some applications. We conjecture that more advanced grooming algorithms might be even more efficient.

Authentication (onte⬜s. We blithely assumed that an attacker is allowed a single guess to produce an absolutely correct answer. Many systems give a user a few tries to allow for mistyping or misremembering before taking draconian measures (such as seizing an ATM card). We conjecture that in many contexts, allowing success on the $+^{th}$ guess increases the probability of success by a factor of at most $+$, so $\log +$ bits should be subtracted from assurance thus attained. We suspect that similarly simple expressions could be found to quantify the assurance of schemes that allow "near" answers, such as one wrong multiple-choice question or missing a character or two in a visual CAPTCHA.

- eal Distributions. Section 6.1 applied grooming to English names. People also tend to remember a variety of other "personal facts" that could be used for authentication, such as telephone numbers, street names and street numbers, postal codes and the like. It would be useful to collect and to analyze such distributions. Dates are particularly interesting. Barring insider information, it seems that the response to the question "my sister's birthday" might have about $\log 365.25$ bits of assurance, even if the attacker could guess the year. The response to " Games and Mary's wedding anniversary" might carry far fewer bits, because of cultural propensities towards "Qne

brides" and weekend weddings (assuming that an attacker could guess the year in question).

Structure of wasswords. Humans tend to compose passwords in predictable fashions. A user might combine a name, a punctuation mark, and a month into the password "ophelia-april". A dog fancier might memorize the personally significant phrase "the best dogs are my 3 Cocker Spaniels at home" and from it derive the password "tbdam3CSQ h". It would be interesting to characterize the assurance in such well-defined password schemes.

Acknowledgments

The authors are grateful for the helpful comments of Henry Baird, Dan Bentley, Qe Hall, David Qfferson and several anonymous referees.

References

Becker, R. A., Q M. Chambers, A. R. Wilks [1988]. *The New S Languagey A wrogramming Environment for Data Analysis and Mraphics*, Wadsworth * Brooks/Cole, Pacific Grove, CA.

Bentley, Q L. and C. L. Mallows [2005]. Problem submitted to *American Mathematical Monthly*.

Bishop, M. and D. V. Klein [1995]. "Improving system security via proactive password checking," *(omputers and Security 1C*, 3, 1995, pp. 233-249.

Cachin, C. [1997]. "Entropy measures and unconditional security in cryptography," Ph.D. Thesis, ETH Zurich.

Chew, M. and H. S. Baird [2003]. "BaffleText: a Human Interactive Proof," *wroceedings ISd TiSwl Document - ecognition and - etrieval ; (onference (E- d - 200T)*, Santa Clara, CA, Qanuary 2003.

Ellison, C., C. Hall, R. Milbert and B. Schneier [2000]. "Protecting secret keys with personal entropy," *Future Meneration (omputer Systems 1A*, 4, February 2000, pp. 311-318.

Feldmeier, D. C. and P.R. Karn [1990]. "UNIX password security – ten years later," *Advances in (ryptology ...(- QvTY 20 wroceedings*, Springer-Verlag, 1990, pp. 44-63.

Knuth, D. E. [1973]. *The Art of (omputer wrogramming, "olume Ty Sorting and Searching*, Addison-Wesley, Reading, MA.

Mauer, U. M. [1996]. "A unified and generalized treatment of authentication theory," *wroc. 1Tth Symposium on Theoretical Aspects of (omputer Science (STA(S TOA)*, Springer-Verlag LCNS 1046, pp. 387-398.

Morris, R. and K. Thompson [1979]. "Password security: A case history," *(omm. A(M 22,*.11, Nov. 1979, pp. 594-597.

O'Gorman, L., A. Bagga, and Q Bentley [2004]. "Call center customer verification by query-directed passwords," *2th Int. Financial (ryptography (onference*, Florida, 9-12 Feb. 2004.

Shannon, C. E. [1948]. "A mathematical theory of communication," *Bell System Tech. L 2R*, Qdly, October, 1948, pp.379-423,623-656, http://cm.bell-labs.com/cm/ms/what/shannonday/paper.html.

Shannon, C. E. [1949]. "Communication theory of secrecy systems," *Bell System Tech. L 22*, October 1949, pp. 656-715.

Smith, R. E. [2002]. *Authentication ...From wasswords to wublic +eys*, Addison-Wesley, Boston, 2002, pp. 87-99.

Wischik, L [1996]. "The Paradox of the Surprise Examination", http://www.wischik.com/lu/philosophy/surprise-exam.html.

Yan, Q, A. Blackwell, R. Anderson, and A. Grant [2000]. "The memorability and security of passwords – some empirical results," TR 500, University of Cambridge, Computer Laboratory, September 2000, http://www.cl.cam.ac.uk/TechReports/UCAM-CL-TR-500.pdf

Phish and HIPs: Human Interactive Proofs to Detect Phishing Attacks

Rachna Dhamija and J.D. Tygar*

University of California, Berkeley
Berkeley, CA 94720
{rachna@sims, tygar@cs}.berkeley.edu

Abstract. In this paper, we propose a new class of Human Interactive
Proofs (HIPs) that allow a human to distinguish one computer from
another. Unlike traditional HIPs, where the computer issues a challenge
to the user over a network, in this case, the user issues a challenge to the
computer. This type of HIP can be used to detect phishing attacks, in
which websites are spoofed in order to trick users into revealing private
information.

We define five properties of an ideal HIP to detect phishing attacks.
Using these properties, we evaluate existing and proposed anti-phishing
schemes to discover their benefits and weaknesses.

We review a new anti-phishing proposal, Dynamic Security Skins (DSS),
and show that it meets the HIP criteria. Our goal is to allow a remote
server to prove its identity in a way that is easy for a human user to
verify and hard for an attacker to spoof. In our scheme, the web server
presents its proof in the form of an image that is unique for each user
and each transaction. To authenticate the server, the user can visually
verify that the image presented by the server matches a reference image
presented by the browser.

1   Introduction

Human Interactive Proofs (HIPs) allow a computer to distinguish a specific class
of humans over a network. HIPs can be designed to distinguish a human from
a computer, one class of humans from another or one particular human from
another human. To do this, the computer presents a challenge that must be easy
for that class of humans to pass, yet hard for non-members to pass. Additionally,
the results must be verifiable by a computer, and the protocol must be publicly
available. [1]

   In this paper, we propose a new class of HIPs that allow a human to distinguish one computer, or computer generated message, from another. Unlike

---

* The authors gratefully acknowledge partial support for this work from the National
Science Foundation and the Unites States Postal Service. The views expressed in
this work are solely those of the authors and do not necessarily reflect the views of
the funding sponsors.

H.S. Baird and D.P. Lopresti (Eds.): HIP 2005, LNCS 3517, pp. 127–141, 2005.

traditional HIPs, where the computer issues a challenge to the user over a network, in this case, the user issues a challenge to the computer. The challenge must:

1. be easy for a particular class of computers to pass,
2. be hard for other computers to pass, even after observing a number of successful authentications,
3. produce results that are easy for a human to verify,
4. use a protocol that is publicly available, and
5. not require the user to have specialized tools.

This class of HIPs can be used by a human to distinguish a known and legitimate website from an unknown one. Such a HIP would be useful in helping humans to detect phishing attacks. In a phishing attack, the attacker spoofs a website (e.g., a financial services website). The attacker draws a victim to a rogue website, sometimes by embedding a link in email and encouraging the user to click on the link. The rogue website usually looks exactly like a known website, sharing logos and images, but the rogue website serves only to capture the users personal information. Many phishing attacks seek to gain credit card information, account numbers, usernames and passwords that enable the attacker to perpetrate fraud and identity theft.

About two million users gave information to spoofed websites resulting in direct losses of \$1.2 billion for U.S. Banks and card issuers in 2003, [2] Some phishing attacks have been able to convince up to 5 percent of their recipients to respond and provide sensitive information. [3] Phishing attacks are successful because current web authentication mechanisms do not meet our third requirement; it is not easy for humans to verify that a successful authentication has taken place.

In Section 2, we present an analysis of authentication and anti-phishing schemes using the HIP criteria. In Section 3, we review a system, Dynamic Security Skins (DSS), that meets the HIP criteria and that allows a remote server to prove its identity by displaying an image to the user. [4] We present our conclusions and future work in Section 4.

2   Analysis of Authentication and Anti-phishing Schemes

2.1   Overview

In this section, we analyze authentication and anti-phishing schemes using the criteria for an ideal HIP. In this class of HIP, the user issues a challenge to the computer. The challenge must:

1. Be easy for a particular class of computers to pass. A scheme can meet this criteria if a specified server can reliably authenticate itself to the user without extraordinary resources.

2. Be hard for other computers to pass. Schemes meet this criteria if it is difficult for illigitimate computers to masquerade as the legitimate server, even after observing a number of successful authentications. Furthermore, it should be hard for illegitimate servers to spoof the indicators of a successful authentication.

3. Produce results that are easy for a human to verify. A user should be able to verify that a successful authentication has taken place, without any undue burden on the user in terms of effort, memory or time. Furthermore, in order to meet this criteria, it must by easy for a user to distinguish the legitimate server from a spoofed server.

4. Use a protocol that is publicly available. We note whether the protocol, technical details, source code or policies of the scheme are publicly available.

5. Not require the user to have specialized tools. We note whether the scheme requires users to have any specialized devices or to store or manage any secrets (e.g., cryptographic keys) in order to successfully verify a legitimate server.

In general, attempts to solve the phishing problem can be divided into three categories: third party certification, direct authentication, and phishing specific tools. In order to discover the benefits and weaknesses of each solution, we analyze them using the HIP criteria discussed above. We discuss our analysis in the next sections, and our results are summarized in Table 1.

2.2   Third Party Certification

Hierarchical Trust Models

SSL/TLS. Public Key Infrastructure (PKI) has long been proposed as a method for users and servers to authenticate each other. In PKI, chains of Certificate Authorities (CAs) vouch for identity by binding a public key to an entity in a digital certificate. The Secure Sockets Layer (SSL) protocol and Transport Layer Security (TLS), its successor, both rely on PKI. SSL/TLS allows a server and client to authenticate each other and to negotiate an encryption algorithm in order to communicate privately.

In the typical use of SSL today, only the server is authenticated, by obtaining an SSL server certificate that is signed by a trusted CA. SSL also supports mutual authentication, where both the client and the server are authenticated, however this mode of operation requires the user to obtain a personal certificate. Though it is an active area of research, there is currently no practical scheme for widely deploying signed personal certificates. A further challenge is how to handle the revocation of credentials. SSL is designed to prevent eavesdropping, tampering, and message forgery in client/server communications. Instead of attacking the protocol, most phishing attacks use very simple spoofing techniques to trick users into believing that their connection is "secure". Some phishing attacks exploit the fact that users can not reliably parse domain names (e.g. they can not distinguish www.paypal.com from www.paypai.com or www.paypal-members-security.com). Many users can not distinguish a legitimate indicator of a secured webpage (e.g. an SSL closed lock icon in the status bar of the browser) from an image of that indicator within the content of a webpage. In many browsers, there is no indicator for "unsecured" sites. This reduces the chance that users will notice spoofed trust indicators when they are inserted into an untrusted page. Other attacks simultaneously display legitimate and illegitimate webpages (e.g., in frames, multiple windows or borderless pop-up windows) in order to trick users into believing that both pages originate from the same website.

It also difficult for users to understand and verify SSL server certificates. Some phishers have gone through the effort of registering a real SSL certificate for their rogue phishing sites that have a similar name to a legitimate site. [5] In order to detect this attack, users must be able to inspect the certificate and to distinguish the domain name of the real website from the rogue site. There are other examples where the CA certificate issuing process has been subverted (e.g., Verisign issued two Class 3 code-signing certificates to an individual who fraudulently claimed to be a Microsoft employee [6]. A user would not be able to detect this attack by inspecting the certificate).

The SSL protocol is publicly available, and the only tool required by the user to authenticate a server is a browser that supports SSL. (To authenticate himself to the server, the user must acquire a personal certificate).

Trustbar. The Trustbar proposal is a third party certification approach that requires website logos to be certified. The authors suggest creating a Trusted Credentials Area (TCA) as a fixed part of the browser window. [7] This area can be used to present credentials from the website, such as logos, icons and seals of the brand that have been certified by trusted certificate authorities or by peers using a PGP web of trust.

The proposal does not specify who will certify logos or how disputes will be resolved in the case of similar logos. If the credentials are signed by trusted CAs, many of the problems of the SSL certificate validation process also apply to this proposal. A strength of this solution is that it does not rely on complex security indicators. However, we expect that all of the spoofing attacks that are common with SSL today will also be applied to the Trustes Credential Area. Because the logos do not change, they can be easily copied and the TCA can be spoofed. An attacker can present an image of the TCA, with the correct logos, in an untrusted page to make it appear legitimate. The success of this attack will depend on the design of the TCA. If there is no visible indicator for unsecured windows, a spoofed TCA may not be detected by users. We expect that phishers will attempt to register logos that can be confused with legitimate logos. Therefore, the strength of this proposal will depend on the strength of the credentials registration process.

The only tool that is required by a user in this scheme is a browser that supports the Trusted Credentials Area.

Table 1. Analysis of authentication and anti-phishing schemes using HIP criteria

Scheme	Easy for specific computer?	Hard for other computers?	Easy for humans to verify?	Protocol available?	Tools required?
SSL	Yes	No	No[1]	Yes	modified browser
Trustbar	Yes	No	No[1]	Yes	modified browser
PGP	Yes	Yes	No[2]	Yes	PGP client/plug-in
3rd Party Seals	Yes	No	No[1]	No	No
AOL Passcode	Yes	No	No[3]	No	SecurID device
SMS Passwords	Yes	No	No[3]	No	cell phone SMS
Passmark	Yes	No	No[4]	No	secure cookie
SRD	Yes	Yes	No[5]	Yes	modified browser
YURL	Yes	No	No[4]	Yes	modified browser
eBay Toolbar	Yes	No	No[1]	No	modified browser
SpoofGuard	Yes	No	No[1]	Yes	modified browser
Spoofstick	Yes	No	No[1]	No	modified browser
DSS	Yes	Yes	Yes[6]	Yes	modified browser

Distributed Trust Models and Third Party Seals

PGP. Another third party approach is the distributed trust model, such as that used by Pretty Good Privacy (PGP). [8] PGP relies on third parties to sign public keys in order to attest that a public key belongs to a particular identity. Unlike centralized PKI schemes, the "web of trust" model relies on individual users to make trust judgments. This allows for more flexibility in how authentication decisions are made, but it requires a great deal of effort on the part of the user to carefully manage keys and to understand the delegation of trust.

It is difficult to break the encryption algorithms, however one simple attack is to create a PGP key using a spoofed identity. Before attesting to a key, users are required to verify the identity of the keyholder (e.g. in a face to face meeting). If users do not take this step before signing a key, an attacker may be able to forge a public key in someone else's name.

Open versions of the PGP protocol are available. In order to authenticate and to verify other parties, the user must have a PGP client application (or a plug-in that implements PGP functionality, which is available for many popular e-mail applications). The user must also store and manage his own private/public key pair and the public keys of others.

---

[1] This scheme is easy to use, but it is hard to distinguish legitimate sites from spoofs.
[2] This scheme is difficult to use.
[3] This scheme requires users to carry a device and does not help users to distinguish legitimate sites from spoofs.
[4] This scheme requires per-site customization by the user.
[5] This scheme employs blinking border windows that may be distracting to users.
[6] See Section 3.

Third Party Seals. Third party seal programs allow one party to certify another party and offer a "seal of approval" that represents this certification. For example, Verisign allows parties that have purchased a Verisign SSL certificate to post a "Secured Seal" on their websites. [9] Visitors can click on the seal to view a VeriSign-generated pop-up window that contains information about the website's SSL certificate and identity. Phishers spoof this seal by copying the image into their own rogue websites. Some phishers also simulate the pop-window by hosting it on their own server, and many users can not detect that window does not originate from Verisign. While many users can recognize the seal, only sophisticated users can distinguish a legitimate seal from an illegitimate one. These weakness also apply to other third party seal programs like TRUSTe. [10]

The criteria for obtaining the seals is publicly available, and no specialized tools are required by the user.

2.3   Direct Authentication

Direct authentication approaches include user authentication, server authentication and mutual authentication schemes.

Multi-factor User Authentication Multi-factor user authentication schemes use a combination of factors to authenticate the user. The factors are "something you know" (e.g., a password or PIN), "something you have" (e.g., a token or key) or "something you are" (e.g., biometrics).

Passcode. America Online's Passcode program has been proposed as a phishing defense. [11, 12] This program distributes RSA SecurID devices to AOL members. The SecureID device generates and displays a unique six-digit numeric code every 60 seconds. To login to the AOL website, the user enters his password and the SecurID code as a secondary password.

This scheme does reduce the value of collecting passwords for attackers because the passwords can not be used for another transaction. It does not, however, prevent a man-in-the-middle (MITM) attack. In this case, the attacker lures a user to a spoofed AOL website to collect both the primary and secondary passwords. The attacker can immediately present the passwords to the AOL website in order to masquerade as the user. The Passcode program does raise the bar for phishing attacks today, because it requires the phishers to immediately use the passwords they collect. However, we expect that if the bar is raised everywhere, this type of live MITM attack will become common.

Because the server is not authenticated, it is difficult for the user to verify if he is interacting with the AOL webpage or a spoofed webpage. There is also no way for AOL to verify if the passwords it receives are from a legitimate user or from an active MITM attack.

The SecurID protocol is not openly available, and this scheme requires the user to carry a SecurID device.

SMS Secondary Passwords. In another two-factor user authentication scheme, a bank delivers a secondary password to the user's cell phone via Simple Messaging Service (SMS).[13] In order to login and to authorize financial transactions, the user must possess his password and the SMS password. Like the AOL passcode scheme, this scheme is designed to protect the server from fraud, rather than protecting the user from phishing attacks. Because the server is not authenticated, it is difficult for the user to determine if he is interacting with a legitimate bank website or a spoofed website.

The security details of this scheme are not openly available, and this scheme requires the user to carry a cell phone that can receive SMS messages.

Server Authentication Using Shared Secrets

Passmark and Verified by Visa. Shared-secret schemes have been proposed as one approach to prevent phishing attacks. In proposals such as Passmark [14] and Verified by Visa [15], the user provides the server with a shared secret, such as an image or passphrase, in addition to his regular password. The server presents the user with this shared secret, and the user is asked to recognize it before providing the server with his password.

The most obvious weakness of this scheme is that the bank must display the shared secret in order to authenticate itself to the user. If the secret is observed or captured, the image can be replayed until the user notices and changes it.

In the Passmark scheme, the bank server places a secure cookie on the user machine, which must be presented at login. This prevents a classic man-in-the-middle (MITM) attack where an attacker interposes himself between the client and the bank. However, a new type of phishing attack is emerging. In this attack, the phisher directs the user to a rogue website, and the users browser opens two windows. The first window displays the real login page of the legitimate bank with legitimate trust indicators (e.g. SSL closed-lock icon, shared secret passmark). The second window displays a webpage from a rogue server. By careful placement of the window, an attacker can convince the user to supply his password. A user may believe that the trust indicators in the first window also apply to the second window, or the user may not even notice that a second window exists.

There is a much easier way to trick the user into revealing his password and passmark. This involves spoofing the Passmark re-registration process. If the user wishes to login using a new browser or a new computer, or if the secure cookie has been deleted, the user must re-register his passmark. Here, the user is shown a "passmark not shown" screen and must enter his password in order to register. This process is inconvenient and also creates a spoofing vulnerabilty. An attacker can direct users to a screen that *claims* that the cookie has been deleted or does not exist. The legitimate Passmark error page asks users to ensure that they have reached the error page by typing in the URL by hand, but a spoofed error page will not include this warning. Spoofing requires no knowledge of the user and requires no special skills other than sending email and creating a website.

A number of attacks are possible that require more difficulty (e.g., breaking the secure cookie, physical observation of the secret image, discovering the potential range of images and then guessing the image). Spoofing is likely to require the least amount of effort to defeat the most people, and we expect that this type of spoofing attack will become common if systems like Passmark are widely deployed.

A final vulnerability of these schemes is that it requires the user to customize each site he wishes to authenticate. The user must be able to recognize the shared secret and associate it with the correct server. Research suggests that users are able to correctly recognize a large number of images. [16] However, if a user is required to remember different images or passphrases for a number of different servers, any difficulty in recognizing an image can be exploited by an attacker.

The security details of the Passmark scheme are not publicly available. This scheme requires the user to store a secure cookie in his browser.

Server Authentication Using Self-shared Secrets These server authentications schemes differ from shared-secret schemes, because an additional secret is shared only with the user's device, rather than shared with a remote server.

Synchronized Random Dynamic Boundaries. Ye and Smith propose "Synchronized Random Dynamic Boundaries" (SRD) to mark authenticated windows in the browser. [17] This scheme uses a random number generator to set a bit that determines the frequency of border changes (i.e., the browser border alternates between an inset and outset position). The user's browser will display authenticated webpages using a border that "blinks" at the correct frequency. The browser will also display the correct blinking pattern in a reference window. Any windows that blink at a different frequency than the reference window can not be trusted.

A strength of this solution is that rogue servers can not predict the random number chosen by the browser, and therefore it is difficult to simulate borders that blink at the correct frequency. Another advantage is that the user simply needs to compare a window border to the reference window in order to verify it. Weaknesses of this approach are that dynamically blinking borders may be annoying and distracting. The security depends on how many border frequency options are available and how many users can correctly distinguish.

The source code for this proposal is publicly available, and the only tool required by a user is a browser that is modified to support SRD.

YURL. In the YURL proposal, the user's browser maintains a mapping of a public key hash to a "petname", or nickname. [18] When a user visits a page identified by a YURL, the browser prominently displays the petname that the user previously associated with the website. An untrusted site can be recognized by the absence of a corresponding petname.

One advantage of this scheme is that the secret (the petname) is shared with the user himself, rather than with the trusted server. Therefore, an attacker must be physically present or must compromise the security of the user's browser or computer to obtain the petname. However, because the secret does not change, it can be replayed if it is captured or observed.

The main disadvantage of the scheme is that it requires user customization for each website (i.e., the user must choose and enter a petname). This scheme relies on user memory to recognize the secret phrase and to associate it with the correct website. Therefore, we expect that that the choice of petname will be predictable. For example, a large subset of users will choose "Amazon" for Amazon.com.

We recommend that designers should not rely on the absence of a pet name to identify untrusted windows. Untrusted windows should be marked in a highly visible way that indicates that no petname is present. Otherwise, attackers can insert an image of the petname display into an untrusted page to fool users (especially those users that choose predictable petnames).

The details of the YURL proposal are publicly available, and the only tool required by the user is a browser modified to display petnames.

2.4   Anti-phishing Tools

eBay Toolbar. The eBay Toolbar is a browser plug-in that eBay offers to its customers, primarily to help them keep track of auction sites. [19] The toolbar has a feature, called "AccountGuard" that monitors the domain names that users visit and provides a warning in the form of a colored tab on the toolbar. The tab is usually grey, but it turns green if the user is on an eBay or PayPal site. It turns red if the user is on a site that is known to be a spoof by eBay. The toolbar also allows users to submit suspected spoof sites to eBay.

Because the colored tab is usually grey, users may ignore this feature in the toolbar. However, once they know about the feature, it is easy to recognize a red-colored tab. This scheme requires no effort on the part of the user, other then to notice color changes in the toolbar.

A drawback to this approach is that it only flags sites that are known to be spoofs by eBay and PayPal. Users are unlikely to install several toolbars that apply to other types of websites (though it may be possible to develop one toolbar that would work for a wider range of sites). The main weakness is that there is always a period of time between the time that a spoof is detected and confirmed and when the toolbar can begin reporting spoofs to users. This will allow some users to view a spoofed page without a warning. If spoof reports are not carefully confirmed, denial of service attacks are possible.

eBay has not revealed the security policies or technical details of the toolbar. The only tool required by the user in this scheme is the browser plug-in supplied by eBay.

SpoofGuard. SpoofGuard is an Internet Explorer browser plug-in that examines web pages and warns users when webpages have a high probability of being spoofs [20]. This calculation is performed by examining the URL, images, and links, comparing them to the stored history and by looking for other characteristics of spoofed sites.

The main weakness of this approach is that the SpoofGuard checks can be evaded by simple modifications to spoof pages. If adopted, SpoofGuard will force phishers to work harder. However, new detection tests must be continuously deployed as phishers become more sophisticated. SpoofGuard makes use of PwdHash [21], an Internet Explorer plug-in that replaces a users password with a one way hash of the password and domain name. As a result, the website only sees the domain specific hash of the password instead of the password itself. This is a simple but useful technique in preventing phishers from collecting user passwords. Unfortunately, it can also create problems where users have multiple accounts at websites with the same domain name, or where account logins occur on pages with different domain names.

This scheme requires no effort on the part of the user other than to notice a status indicator (a red, yellow or green light on the toolbar) and view warning windows (which can optionally be turned off). No additional tools other than a browser plug-in are required.

Spoofstick. Spoofstick is a simple toolbar extension for the Internet Explorer and Mozilla Firefox browsers. [22] The toolbar provides basic information about the domain name of the website. For example, if the user is visiting Ebay, the toolbar displays "You're on ebay.com". If the user is at a spoofed site, the toolbar might instead display "You're on 10.19.32.4". This toolbar can help the user to detect phishing attacks where phishers choose domain names that are syntactically or semantically similar to a legitimate domain name.

Spoofstick is vulnerable to a phishing attack where different websites are opened in multiple frames in the browser window. Spoofstick may display the correct domain name from the legitimate site in one frame, while the user is viewing a site hosted by a rogue server in another frame.

This scheme requires only requires that the user check the domain name listed in the toolbar. It allows the user to customize the appearance of the toolbar, which prevents the toolbar itself from being spoofed (e.g. from being displayed as a static image within the content of an untrusted page).

The technical details of the operation of the toolbar are not publicly available. The user requires no additional tools other than the browser plugin.

3   Dynamic Security Skins

We evaluate a system that we recently proposed, Dynamic Security Skins (DSS). DSS allows a remote server to prove its identity in a way that is easy for a human user to verify and hard for an attacker to spoof[4]. We are implementing DSS as an extension for the Mozilla Firefox browser. Here we briefly review the system with respect to the HIP criteria.

Our extension provides the user with a *trusted password window*. This is a dedicated window for the user to enter usernames and passwords and for the browser to display security information. We establish a trusted path to the password window by assigning each user a random photographic image that will always appear in that window. The user should easily be able to recognize the personal photo and should only enter his password when this image is displayed. As shown in Figure 1, the photographic image serves as the background of the window, and it is also transparently overlaid onto the textboxes. This ensures that user focus is on the image at the point of text entry and makes it more difficult to spoof the password entry boxes (e.g., by using a pop-up window over that area).

Fig. 1. The trusted password window uses a background image to prevent spoofing of the window and textboxes

We adapt an existing protocol, the Secure Remote Password protocol (SRP) developed by Tom Wu [23], that allows a user and server to authenticate each other over an untrusted network. We chose SRP because it allows us to preserve the familiar use of passwords, without requiring the user to send his password to the server. Instead, the user chooses a password and then applies a one-way function to that secret to generate a *verifier*. The user sends the verifier to the server one time. After the first exchange, the user and the server engage in a series of steps that prove to each other that they hold the verifier, without revealing it. The protocol resists dictionary attacks on the verifier from both passive and active attackers, which allows weak passwords to be used safely.

Assuming that a successful authentication has taken place, how can a user distinguish authenticated web pages from those that are not "secure"? To accomplish this, we adapted the SRP protocol (use of this specific protocol is not a requirement for our approach). In the last step of the protocol, the server presents a proof to the user in the form of a hash value. In our system, the server uses the hash value to generate an abstract image, or *visual hash*. [24] As a visual hash algorithm, we use Random Art [13], which has previously been proposed for use in graphical password user authentication. [24, 25, 26] The remote server can use the image to create a "skin" that modifies the appearance

Fig. 2. The trusted password window displays a visual hash that should match the website image

Fig. 3. The remote website displays a visual hash in the background of a form

of the webpage or particular elements in a web page (e.g., an image can be embedded in a web form that requests sensitive information). The user's browser can independently compute the same image because it also knows the values of the verifier and random parameters that were exchanged by each party during the protocol. The browser presents the user with the image that it expects to receive from the server in the trusted window. If the website image matches the image displayed in the user's trusted window, the user can easily verify that the information request originates from a known party. DSS meets the criteria for a HIP that allows humans to detect phishing attacks. In our system, the user issues a challenge to the server that is:

1. Is easy for a legitimate computer to pass. A legitimate server that holds the user's verifier can display the correct visual hash on its website.
2. Is hard for other computers to pass. A rogue server can not produce a visual hash that will match the users reference image without the user verifier. If the visual hash image is observed or captured, it can not be replayed in subsequent transactions. If users can recognize his personal image, the trusted window is hard to spoof.
3. Produces results that are easy for a human to verify. Creating a trusted path to the password window requires no effort (or a one-time customization for users who wish to change personal images). The user must only recognize one image to verify the trusted window and visually match two images to establish the identity of the server.
4. Uses a protocol that is publicly available. The security of DSS does not rely on the secrecy of the browser or source code or browser extension source code, and the SRP protocol is publicly available.
5. Does not require the user to have specialized tools. DSS requires the user to have a browser that includes our extension. It does not require the user to store or manage any keys. The only secret that must be available to the browser is the user password (that can be a weak password memorized by the user).

4   Conclusions and Future Work

In this paper, we propose a new class of HIPs that allow a human to distinguish one computer from another. In this type of HIP, the user presents a challenge that must be easy for a particular computer to pass, yet hard for other computers to pass. Additionally, the results must be verifiable by a human, and the protocol must be publicly available. This class of HIPs can be used by a human to distinguish a known and legitimate website from an unknown one in order to detect phishing attacks.

We define five properties of an ideal HIP to detect phishing attacks. Using these properties, we evaluate existing and proposed anti-phishing schemes to discover their benefits and weaknesses.

We evaluate a recently proposed system that allows a remote server to prove its identity in a way that is easy for a human user to verify and hard for an attacker to spoof. In our scheme, the server presents its proof in the form of an image that is unique for each user and each transaction. The user's browser can independently compute the image that it expects to receive from the server. To authenticate the server, the user can visually verify that the images match.

We will continue development of the prototype and will conduct a user study to evaluate the effectiveness of image comparison as a technique for users to identify remote servers. In the user study, we will test whether users can reliably recognize their trusted window and whether they can be fooled by spoofed trusted windows and spoofed server images.

References

[1] First Workshop on Human Interactive Proofs. `http://www2.parc.com/istl/groups/did/HIP2002/` (2002)

[2] Litan, A.: Phishing Attack Victims Likely Targets for Identity Theft. Gartner Research FT-22-8873 (2004)

[3] Loftesness, S.: Responding to Phishing Attacks. `http://www.glenbrook.com/opinions/phishing.htm` (2004)

[4] Dhamija, R., Tygar, J.D.: (Phishing: A Model Problem for Usability in Privacy and Security (To Appear))

[5] Netcraft: SSLs Credibility as Phishing Defense is Tested. `http://news.netcraft.com/archives/2004/03/08/ssls_credibility_as_phishing_defense_is_tested.html` (2004)

[6] Microsoft: Erroneous Verisign Issued Digital Certificates Pose Spoofing Hazard. Technical Report Microsoft Security Bulletin MS01-017 (2001)

[7] Herzberg, A., Gbara, A.: Protecting (even) Naive Web Users, or: Preventing Spoofing and Establishing Credentials of Websites. Technical Report Draft of July 2004 (2004)

[8] Pretty Good Privacy. (`www.pgp.com/`)

[9] Verisign: Verisign Secured Seal Program. (`http://www.verisign.com/products-services/security-services/secured-seal/`)

[10] TRUSTe. (`http://www.truste.org/`)

[11] RSA Security: America Online and RSA Security Launch AOL PassCode Premium Service. `http://www.rsasecurity.com/press_release.asp?doc_id=5033` (2004)

[12] RSA Security: Protecting Against Phishing by Implementing Strong Two-Factor Authentication. `https://www.rsasecurity.com/products/securid/whitepapers/PHISH_WP_0904.pdf` (2004)

[13] Pullar-Strecker, T.: NZ bank adds security online. (The Sydney Morning Herald, November 8, 2004)

[14] Passmark Security: Protecting Your Customers from Phishing Attacks: an Introduction to Passmarks. (`http://www.passmarksecurity.com/`)

[15] Visa USA: Verified by Visa. (`https://usa.visa.com/personal/security/vbv/`)

[16] Haber, R.N.: How We Remember What We See. Scientific American **222** (1970) 104–112

[17] Zishuang, Y., Smith, S.: Trusted Paths for Browsers. In: Proceedings of the 11th USENIX Security Symposium,, IEEE Computer Society Press (2002)

[18] Waterken Inc.: Waterken YURL Trust Management for Humans. `http://www.waterken.com/dev/YURL/Name/` (2004)

[19] eBay: eBay Toolbar. (`http://pages.ebay.com/ebay_toolbar/`)

[20] Chou, N., Ledesma, R., Teraguchi, Y., Boneh, D., Mitchell, J.C.: Client Side Defense Against Web-based Identity Theft. (`http://crypto.stanford.edu/SpoofGuard/`)

[21] Ross, B., Jackson, C., Miyake, N., Boneh, D., Mitchell, J.C.: A Browser Plug-in Solution to the Unique Password Problem. Technical Report Stanford-SecLab-TR-2005-1 (2005)

[22] Core Street: SpoofStick. (`www.corestreet.com/spoofstick/`)

[23] Wu, T.: The Secure Remote Password Protocol. In: Proceedings of the 1998 Internet Society Network and Distributed System Security Symposium, San Diego, CA. (1998)

[24] Perrig, A., Song, D.: Hash Visualization: A New Technique to Improve Real World Security. In: International Workshop on Cryptographic Techniques and E-Commerce. (1999)

[25] Dhamija, R.: Hash Visualization in User Authentication. In: Proceedings of the Computer Human Interaction Conference Short Papers. (2000)

[26] Dhamija, R., Perrig, A.: Déjà Vu: A User Study. Using Images for Authentication. In: Proceedings of the 9th USENIX Security Symposium. (2000)

Author Index

Baird, H.S., 27
Bentley, J., 111

Chellapilla, K., 1
Chew, M., 66
Converse, T., 82
Czerwinski, M., 1

Dhamija, R., 127

Govindaraju, V., 42

Janke, G., 53

Kallin, S., 53

Larson, K., 1
Liu, Z., 53
Lopresti, D., 97

Mallows, C., 111
Moll, M.A., 27

Paya, C., 53

Rui, Y., 53
Rusu, A., 42

Simard, P.Y., 1

Tygar, J.D., 66, 127

Wang, S.-Y., 27

Lecture Notes in Computer Science

For information about Vols. 1–3379

please contact your bookseller or Springer

Vol. 3525: A.E. Abdallah, C.B. Jones, J.W. Sanders (Eds.), Communicating Sequential Processes. XIV, 321 pages. 2005.

Vol. 3517: H.S. Baird, D.P. Lopresti (Eds.), Human Interactive Proofs. IX, 143 pages. 2005.

Vol. 3510: T. Braun, G. Carle, Y. Koucheryavy, V. Tsaoussidis (Eds.), Wired/Wireless Internet Communications. XIV, 366 pages. 2005.

Vol. 3508: P. Bresciani, P. Giorgini, B. Henderson-Sellers, G. Low, M. Winikoff (Eds.), Agent-Oriented Information Systems II. X, 227 pages. 2005. (Subseries LNAI).

Vol. 3503: S.E. Nikoletseas (Ed.), Experimental and Efficient Algorithms. XV, 624 pages. 2005.

Vol. 3501: B. Kégl, G. Lapalme (Eds.), Advances in Artificial Intelligence. XV, 458 pages. 2005. (Subseries LNAI).

Vol. 3500: S. Miyano, J. Mesirov, S. Kasif, S. Istrail, P. Pevzner, M. Waterman (Eds.), Research in Computational Molecular Biology. XVII, 632 pages. 2005. (Subseries LNBI).

Vol. 3498: J. Wang, X. Liao, Z. Yi (Eds.), Advances in Neural Networks – ISNN 2005, Part III. L, 1077 pages. 2005.

Vol. 3497: J. Wang, X. Liao, Z. Yi (Eds.), Advances in Neural Networks – ISNN 2005, Part II. L, 947 pages. 2005.

Vol. 3496: J. Wang, X. Liao, Z. Yi (Eds.), Advances in Neural Networks – ISNN 2005, Part II. L, 1055 pages. 2005.

Vol. 3495: P. Kantor, G. Muresan, F. Roberts, D.D. Zeng, F.-Y. Wang, H. Chen, R.C. Merkle (Eds.), Intelligence and Security Informatics. XVIII, 674 pages. 2005.

Vol. 3494: R. Cramer (Ed.), Advances in Cryptology – EUROCRYPT 2005. XIV, 576 pages. 2005.

Vol. 3492: P. Blache, E. Stabler, J. Busquets, R. Moot (Eds.), Logical Aspects of Computational Linguistics. X, 363 pages. 2005. (Subseries LNAI).

Vol. 3489: G.T. Heineman, J.A. Stafford, H.W. Schmidt, K. Wallnau, C. Szyperski, I. Crnkovic (Eds.), Component-Based Software Engineering. XI, 358 pages. 2005.

Vol. 3488: M.-S. Hacid, N.V. Murray, Z.W. Raś, S. Tsumoto (Eds.), Foundations of Intelligent Systems. XIII, 700 pages. 2005. (Subseries LNAI).

Vol. 3467: J. Giesl (Ed.), Term Rewriting and Applications. XIII, 517 pages. 2005.

Vol. 3465: M. Bernardo, A. Bogliolo (Eds.), Formal Methods for Mobile Computing. VII, 271 pages. 2005.

Vol. 3463: M. Dal Cin, M. Kaâniche, A. Pataricza (Eds.), Dependable Computing - EDCC 2005. XVI, 472 pages. 2005.

Vol. 3462: R. Boutaba, K. Almeroth, R. Puigjaner, S. Shen, J.P. Black (Eds.), NETWORKING 2005. XXX, 1483 pages. 2005.

Vol. 3461: P. Urzyczyn (Ed.), Typed Lambda Calculi and Applications. XI, 433 pages. 2005.

Vol. 3459: R. Kimmel, N.A. Sochen, J. Weickert (Eds.), Scale Space and PDE Methods in Computer Vision. XI, 634 pages. 2005.

Vol. 3456: H. Rust, Operational Semantics for Timed Systems. XII, 223 pages. 2005.

Vol. 3455: H. Treharne, S. King, M. Henson, S. Schneider (Eds.), ZB 2005: Formal Specification and Development in Z and B. XV, 493 pages. 2005.

Vol. 3454: J.-M. Jacquet, G.P. Picco (Eds.), Coordination Models and Languages. X, 299 pages. 2005.

Vol. 3453: L. Zhou, B.C. Ooi, X. Meng (Eds.), Database Systems for Advanced Applications. XXVII, 929 pages. 2005.

Vol. 3452: F. Baader, A. Voronkov (Eds.), Logic for Programming, Artificial Intelligence, and Reasoning. XI, 562 pages. 2005. (Subseries LNAI).

Vol. 3450: D. Hutter, M. Ullmann (Eds.), Security in Pervasive Computing. XI, 239 pages. 2005.

Vol. 3449: F. Rothlauf, J. Branke, S. Cagnoni, D.W. Corne, R. Drechsler, Y. Jin, P. Machado, E. Marchiori, J. Romero, G.D. Smith, G. Squillero (Eds.), Applications of Evolutionary Computing. XX, 631 pages. 2005.

Vol. 3448: G.R. Raidl, J. Gottlieb (Eds.), Evolutionary Computation in Combinatorial Optimization. XI, 271 pages. 2005.

Vol. 3447: M. Keijzer, A. Tettamanzi, P. Collet, J.v. Hemert, M. Tomassini (Eds.), Genetic Programming. XIII, 382 pages. 2005.

Vol. 3444: M. Sagiv (Ed.), Programming Languages and Systems. XIII, 439 pages. 2005.

Vol. 3443: R. Bodik (Ed.), Compiler Construction. XI, 305 pages. 2005.

Vol. 3442: M. Cerioli (Ed.), Fundamental Approaches to Software Engineering. XIII, 373 pages. 2005.

Vol. 3441: V. Sassone (Ed.), Foundations of Software Science and Computational Structures. XVIII, 521 pages. 2005.

Vol. 3440: N. Halbwachs, L.D. Zuck (Eds.), Tools and Algorithms for the Construction and Analysis of Systems. XVII, 588 pages. 2005.

Vol. 3439: R.H. Deng, F. Bao, H. Pang, J. Zhou (Eds.), Information Security Practice and Experience. XII, 424 pages. 2005.

Vol. 3437: T. Gschwind, C. Mascolo (Eds.), Software Engineering and Middleware. X, 245 pages. 2005.

Vol. 3436: B. Bouyssounouse, J. Sifakis (Eds.), Embedded Systems Design. XV, 492 pages. 2005.

Vol. 3434: L. Brun, M. Vento (Eds.), Graph-Based Representations in Pattern Recognition. XII, 384 pages. 2005.

Vol. 3433: S. Bhalla (Ed.), Databases in Networked Information Systems. VII, 319 pages. 2005.

Vol. 3432: M. Beigl, P. Lukowicz (Eds.), Systems Aspects in Organic and Pervasive Computing - ARCS 2005. X, 265 pages. 2005.

Vol. 3431: C. Dovrolis (Ed.), Passive and Active Network Measurement. XII, 374 pages. 2005.

Vol. 3429: E. Andres, G. Damiand, P. Lienhardt (Eds.), Discrete Geometry for Computer Imagery. X, 428 pages. 2005.

Vol. 3427: G. Kotsis, O. Spaniol (Eds.), Wireless Systems and Mobility in Next Generation Internet. VIII, 249 pages. 2005.

Vol. 3423: J.L. Fiadeiro, P.D. Mosses, F. Orejas (Eds.), Recent Trends in Algebraic Development Techniques. VIII, 271 pages. 2005.

Vol. 3422: R.T. Mittermeir (Ed.), From Computer Literacy to Informatics Fundamentals. X, 203 pages. 2005.

Vol. 3421: P. Lorenz, P. Dini (Eds.), Networking - ICN 2005, Part II. XXXV, 1153 pages. 2005.

Vol. 3420: P. Lorenz, P. Dini (Eds.), Networking - ICN 2005, Part I. XXXV, 933 pages. 2005.

Vol. 3419: B. Faltings, A. Petcu, F. Fages, F. Rossi (Eds.), Constraint Satisfaction and Constraint Logic Programming. X, 217 pages. 2005. (Subseries LNAI).

Vol. 3418: U. Brandes, T. Erlebach (Eds.), Network Analysis. XII, 471 pages. 2005.

Vol. 3416: M. Böhlen, J. Gamper, W. Polasek, M.A. Wimmer (Eds.), E-Government: Towards Electronic Democracy. XIII, 311 pages. 2005. (Subseries LNAI).

Vol. 3415: P. Davidsson, B. Logan, K. Takadama (Eds.), Multi-Agent and Multi-Agent-Based Simulation. X, 265 pages. 2005. (Subseries LNAI).

Vol. 3414: M. Morari, L. Thiele (Eds.), Hybrid Systems: Computation and Control. XII, 684 pages. 2005.

Vol. 3412: X. Franch, D. Port (Eds.), COTS-Based Software Systems. XVI, 312 pages. 2005.

Vol. 3411: S.H. Myaeng, M. Zhou, K.-F. Wong, H.-J. Zhang (Eds.), Information Retrieval Technology. XIII, 337 pages. 2005.

Vol. 3410: C.A. Coello Coello, A. Hernández Aguirre, E. Zitzler (Eds.), Evolutionary Multi-Criterion Optimization. XVI, 912 pages. 2005.

Vol. 3409: N. Guelfi, G. Reggio, A. Romanovsky (Eds.), Scientific Engineering of Distributed Java Applications. X, 127 pages. 2005.

Vol. 3408: D.E. Losada, J.M. Fernández-Luna (Eds.), Advances in Information Retrieval. XVII, 572 pages. 2005.

Vol. 3407: Z. Liu, K. Araki (Eds.), Theoretical Aspects of Computing - ICTAC 2004. XIV, 562 pages. 2005.

Vol. 3406: A. Gelbukh (Ed.), Computational Linguistics and Intelligent Text Processing. XVII, 829 pages. 2005.

Vol. 3404: V. Diekert, B. Durand (Eds.), STACS 2005. XVI, 706 pages. 2005.

Vol. 3403: B. Ganter, R. Godin (Eds.), Formal Concept Analysis. XI, 419 pages. 2005. (Subseries LNAI).

Vol. 3402: M. Daydé, J.J. Dongarra, V. Hernández, J.M.L.M. Palma (Eds.), High Performance Computing for Computational Science - VECPAR 2004. XI, 732 pages. 2005.

Vol. 3401: Z. Li, L.G. Vulkov, J. Waśniewski (Eds.), Numerical Analysis and Its Applications. XIII, 630 pages. 2005.

Vol. 3399: Y. Zhang, K. Tanaka, J.X. Yu, S. Wang, M. Li (Eds.), Web Technologies Research and Development - APWeb 2005. XXII, 1082 pages. 2005.

Vol. 3398: D.-K. Baik (Ed.), Systems Modeling and Simulation: Theory and Applications. XIV, 733 pages. 2005. (Subseries LNAI).

Vol. 3397: T.G. Kim (Ed.), Artificial Intelligence and Simulation. XV, 711 pages. 2005. (Subseries LNAI).

Vol. 3396: R.M. van Eijk, M.-P. Huget, F. Dignum (Eds.), Agent Communication. X, 261 pages. 2005. (Subseries LNAI).

Vol. 3395: J. Grabowski, B. Nielsen (Eds.), Formal Approaches to Software Testing. X, 225 pages. 2005.

Vol. 3394: D. Kudenko, D. Kazakov, E. Alonso (Eds.), Adaptive Agents and Multi-Agent Systems II. VIII, 313 pages. 2005. (Subseries LNAI).

Vol. 3393: H.-J. Kreowski, U. Montanari, F. Orejas, G. Rozenberg, G. Taentzer (Eds.), Formal Methods in Software and Systems Modeling. XXVII, 413 pages. 2005.

Vol. 3392: D. Seipel, M. Hanus, U. Geske, O. Bartenstein (Eds.), Applications of Declarative Programming and Knowledge Management. X, 309 pages. 2005. (Subseries LNAI).

Vol. 3391: C. Kim (Ed.), Information Networking. XVII, 936 pages. 2005.

Vol. 3390: R. Choren, A. Garcia, C. Lucena, A. Romanovsky (Eds.), Software Engineering for Multi-Agent Systems III. XII, 291 pages. 2005.

Vol. 3389: P. Van Roy (Ed.), Multiparadigm Programming in Mozart/Oz. XV, 329 pages. 2005.

Vol. 3388: J. Lagergren (Ed.), Comparative Genomics. VII, 133 pages. 2005. (Subseries LNBI).

Vol. 3387: J. Cardoso, A. Sheth (Eds.), Semantic Web Services and Web Process Composition. VIII, 147 pages. 2005.

Vol. 3386: S. Vaudenay (Ed.), Public Key Cryptography - PKC 2005. IX, 436 pages. 2005.

Vol. 3385: R. Cousot (Ed.), Verification, Model Checking, and Abstract Interpretation. XII, 483 pages. 2005.

Vol. 3383: J. Pach (Ed.), Graph Drawing. XII, 536 pages. 2005.

Vol. 3382: J. Odell, P. Giorgini, J.P. Müller (Eds.), Agent-Oriented Software Engineering V. X, 239 pages. 2005.

Vol. 3381: P. Vojtáš, M. Bieliková, B. Charron-Bost, O. Sýkora (Eds.), SOFSEM 2005: Theory and Practice of Computer Science. XV, 448 pages. 2005.

Vol. 3380: C. Priami (Ed.), Transactions on Computational Systems Biology I. IX, 111 pages. 2005. (Subseries LNBI).